L. 'Deeno' Longstaff: 1924 - 2007

"And not by eastern windows only.
When daylight comes, comes in the light.
In front, the sun climbs slow, how slowly.
But westward, look, the land is bright!"
A.H. Clough.

The Land is Bright.

by
Lavender Dixon Longstaff

From here

Twitchen House, North Devon, England

Copyright © 2016,
Timothy Harold Birmingham.
All Rights Reserved.
With thanks to Ian Hutton.
ISBN# 987-0-9950335-2-8

To here

My cabin, Salmon Arm, BC, Canada

THE LAND IS BRIGHT

All Aboard.

Forests, forests, and more forests. Now I knew the meaning of the term virgin forest, now I began to realize something of Canada's vastness. Long before dawn, one could pick out, against the night sky a silhouette of gentle birch and sharp spruce-tips, and in the train's dim lights blurred branches and rocky banks loomed up in endless procession. More sleep, then trees again, trees and rocks, trees and rocks; now and again a wall of stony embankment would hide them, but always the forest would return. More sleep, then a glorious, unforgettable moment: An opening in the wall of trees, a rocky waste, then, all unsuspected, there was an open lake, framed with jagged bare rock headlands and filled with the pale serenity of a dawn sky. More rocks, more trees, and the lake is gone. Another bend, and it is in view again in its full glory, a mile of shining rock-bound water, alone, unspoilt.

I wanted to rush and tell everyone: look, quick, see what I have found! See what you are missing, all of you, snoring with your blinds drawn stuffily down! But, alas, one cannot do such things. The lake receded, blotted out by more trees; but soon I learned to watch for gaps in the tree-top line, and to sit up at each one of them to catch sight of a new lake, and another, and another. Some were big, some mere ponds, but all were framed with the same naked red-brown rock and scrubby trees; and each one mirrored a brighter dawn sky till at last the sun rose over the trees into blue day.

Soon we were out of this Canadian version of a Lake District: now and again a single, much bigger lake would glide slowly past the window; then nothing but trees. Yes, the forest persisted, more and more and, incredibly, more of it. All through that day, all through the long hours of another night, and well into the next morning, the train was to rush on and on, on and on, still hemmed in on either side by a bank of soft green birch and ragged, dark little spruce trees, with a carpet of scrubby undergrowth and big stones.

So filled was I with wonder, thinking of the hundreds of miles of this same forest which must stretch away from us to the north and south from any point along the track, that I never imagined I could actually see too much of it! That on waking next morning, sitting up with happy anticipation, I would only need one glimpse of those raggedy- jaggedy thin black spruce-tops to send me snuggling back into my pillows with a grunt of disgust.

I was rushing through all these forests for no other reason than that I wanted to go west. In fact, I had to go west: nothing else in life mattered but that I must see British Columbia. Oh, I knew now how the migrating swallows felt, and the wild geese flying northwards! Back in Toronto, the dry old spinsters in the office couldn't see the point at all: "Oh, you can have the West!" said they, scornfully. "Have you ever been there?" I asked. "No, and we don't want to." Well, I should have the West! I should see real mountains at last, mile upon mile of soaring peaks, green and white glaciers, foaming rivers. I should work on a farm by a green lake ringed with mountains; their snowy peaks would glow with pink in the sunset, and their lower slopes would be covered with forests where I could roam at will. No more fenced-off farmlands and nicely laid out picnicking parks for me. I was going to gaze my fill at the mountains, and become enchanted with chipmunks.... I was not guessing, I was not dreaming: I knew. Without a doubt, I knew!

I was baby-sitting near Toronto, looking after my sister's family while she spent a month at home in England , when the idea was born. It had been growing in my mind long before that, nourished by scattered experiences and by other people. By an aerial photograph of the Canadian Rockies in a big Country Life book, in England long ago. By the simple families with their soft drawling accents and unspoilt characters, blue- jeaned, check-shirted, living in warm wooden cabins in the loveliest places – the people of the best Western films who had captured my imagination

I wanted to meet them, to be them! By the English doctor I met on the Atlantic crossing, who understood me well enough to know that British Columbia would be the place for me, and lost no time in telling so: he showed me maps, told me of the mountains, of Vancouver City, of the farms in the Fraser Valley. "It is their whole way of life, their attitude, that I liked so much, and that you would like too," he said. "It is hard to put it into words. Well, it's like this: a farmer can work all day with you and then sit down under a haystack and talk philosophy. Do you see what I mean?" I saw exactly what he meant, and from that moment I knew that I should be happy in British Columbia.

Rosie and John (my sister and son)

Then there was Harry, my sister's next-door neighbour, without whose encouragement I should perhaps never have taken the plunge. Harry was gentle and kind, and so alive mentally that he could stimulate even me to fresh interests in life. I, being tired, busy and bored all at once, and feeling hemmed in with domestic chores and two small nephews, had been day-dreaming, and I happened to mention my day-dreams to Harry one day. "Harry, do you know what I've been thinking? This is such a beautifully free country, no rationing, no trouble with emergency cards, no red tape and no questions asked, hotels easy to get into....I have been imagining myself, only imagining, mind you, going off to B.C. on my own! Not planning ahead at all, but just taking what luggage I could carry, and getting off the train at the first place that took my fancy. Wouldn't it be fun? I'd find a job – farming, fruit picking, anything, and if I didn't like one place I would move on...." Harry broke into my dream, all enthusiasm. "Well why don't you?" he said .So the idea was born, we discussed it and I took the decision.

After the decision, there was Driftwood Valley . My brother-in-law went to the Toronto library to find me any books they had on British Columbia, and brought back Driftwood Valley, by Theodora C. Stanwell-Fletcher. I scanned the exquisite pencil drawings of animals, shuddered pleasurably at the timber wolf and completely fell for the grey chipmunk, who held his tail straight up like a cat's and ate soft grey pussy willow catkins which he held in his front paws. Then I read the text and grew to love the two people who built their log cabin in the wild North, and who walked for hours through the forest and over the mountains in silence because they loved the place and loved each other and felt no need for words. With them I went on snowshoes behind the sled-dogs at temperatures of around forty below; with them I sweltered in the summer heat, tormented by mosquitoes; with them I met wolves and bears, eagles and hummingbirds, with them I knew lakes and mountains and forest trails, and found that life was good. To make this wonderful book last longer I read only a couple of pages each night, and when it was over I could hardly wait to be off West myself.

CHAPTER TWO

So strong had been the westward urge that this journey of mine seemed almost inevitable, and I had embarked upon it with a strange lack of emotion. I had an extraordinary sensation: I felt as though it were a book already written, and I had to live through it. At midnight the previous night, at Toronto Union Station, I had set off on the adventure of my dreams (my family back in England called it my Great Western Adventure) : surely a great moment in my life. But, as happens so often at great moments, I felt nothing at the time, and noticed only prosaic little details. I am sorry to say I felt no sisterly regrets; and I had not the least apprehension about this three- thousand- mile journey into the blue, just as if I travelled across Canada every week!

My sister had by that time returned from England, and she and her husband treated me to a grand farewell dinner, with champagne, in Toronto. By midnight I had drifted into a state of suspended animation, living entirely in the present. I could not realise what I was leaving; and, when my brother-in-law and sister said goodbye, I was conscious only of the effort of remembering all the proper last-minute things to say.

Neither did I think of what lay ahead of me, beyond the immediate delights of the train itself. This was my first close-up view of one of the huge Canadian trains. It towered over us, metallic and impersonal yet throbbing with urgency and the promise of great distances. At least half of it seemed to consist of a black complication of wheels, pipes, and undercarriage: the shiny, brown paint and long, clean windows occupied only an insignificant strip along the top. Way down below each door, a "footstool" was placed on the ground, and by each "footstool" stood a coloured porter in an immaculate white coat, waiting to help one up the steep steps. Canada does not have station platforms – not even in Toronto.

This was my first experience of sleeping-cars; I was having such an orgy of first experiences that I was soon exhausted. At last I sank blissfully into a comfortable, springy mattress, enclosed in my own private, curtained cubby-hole, and was rocked by the train to an untroubled sleep. Next morning - the morning of Tuesday , May 23rd, 1950 – I found myself gazing at the limitless forest of Northern Ontario: gazing with delight, then with growing wonder, and finally with impatience. But, fortunately, the scenery is not the only joy of a journey. I had plenty of other diversions, beginning with the difficulties of dressing horizontally, washing in tepid water with no space or privacy, and tidying hair, face and possessions in the cramped but private green- curtained box that was to be my bedroom for two more nights. I loved that bedroom already, it was not only the first I had had for weeks, but, unlike most bedrooms, it had a magic window with a new selection of views each morning.

At breakfast my table-companion was a pleasant girl from Vancouver, who introduced herself as Janet, and invited me to come to the Observation Car with her afterwards. We sat there all the morning in such luxury that I began to feel guilty, and to suspect that this Observation Car was forbidden to tourist class passengers like myself. We read magazines, talked a little, and both covertly noticed our fellow passengers, who were mostly men. There was an old man writing at a desk; and several raw young students, all wearing blazers with University badges, who came in and out in groups, talking and laughing hilariously. Only one figure attracted my attention: a young giant of a man wearing dark glassed and reading quietly in an armchair. He too wore a blazer, but without a badge; he seemed more mature than the others. I liked his long, serious face, and the shape of his head; and I found myself wishing he would take off the dark glasses so that I could see his eyes. But after a while he got up and walked out, and I took up another magazine.

After lunching with Janet, I returned to Tourist Car No. 71 to find my curtained bed miraculously transformed to two seats, containing my possessions and a young man bound for Calgary, who had evidently slept long and late in the birth over mine. This new companion seemed quite impressed when he heard that I was going to British Columbia without knowing a soul there. "That takes a bit of gumption," he said. Heartwarming words! I felt quite the brave pioneer. Soon I took my writing case and set off once again for the Observation Car. I passed through several tourist cars and three first class ones and it struck me that there was very little difference between the two classes. Both had comfortable looking seats, clean white pillows and little tables. Each person had two seats to himself, and all the cars were air-conditioned and spotlessly clean. Janet was sitting in her first class seat and I stopped to talk with her there; then I staggered on down the swaying train, through the kitchen, through the long empty Dining Car, past odd little doors marked "Drawing Room" and "Roomette." At long last I arrived in the Observation Car, where I settled down to writing and reading all afternoon.

I wrote a long letter home: " What you call my Great Western Adventure had well and truly begun! And even now, I don't think I have fully realized it. At present I am sitting in luxurious comfort in the Observation Car at the back, where I believe I have no business whatever, with only a tourist ticket. But nobody seems to notice, so here I stay! It is like a long lounge, with nice comfortable armchairs and little tables real proper furniture, as movable as the furniture in a hotel lounge. On both sides and across the back are big clear windows for the enthusiastic observers to look out of; while on the tables are good magazines, and even good books, for the bored observers to look into. " In my own car it is stiflingly hot, and the lavatory and washroom are appalling; while here it is cool and comfortable and the modern conveniences leave nothing to be desired. Yet at present there are only four other people in here. It is worth breaking the rules for the sake of coolness: I shall get no proper wash till 48 hours from now.

" Outside are endless, endless miles of what one normally thinks of as typical Canada: virgin forest (mostly spruce and birch), bare rocks, and countless sparkling blue lakes, and, just very occasionally, a village consisting of a few wooden shacks. That is what we have been going through since I woke at about 4 a.m., and it is now 2:30 p.m.. You just cannot conceive what a vast amount of wilderness there is.

" Here in Northern Ontario, the trees are still bare, fat grey pussy-willows being the only signs of Spring; yet near Toronto the trees were already green, and it was hot enough for picnics and sunbathing. We have just passed a big lake half full of snow, or melting ice, or something surprisingly wintry.

" It is now nearly 4 p.m., and we are still racing through exactly the same type of country; I don't think we have passed a sign of human habitation since before I began this letter at 2:30. I am beginning to have a very great respect for the pioneers who laid this railway down. Now I am going to read; I will finish this tonight."

I read my book desultorily for a while, but could not concentrate on it. I felt I had to keep looking out of the window, just in case there should be a change of scenery. Not a hope! The conductor was sitting over in the corner, and I kept catching his eye: the less I meant to, the more it happened. I did not know whether to be pleased or annoyed; one moment I liked his face and the next I was suspicious. However, in the end he came and talked to me and proved pleasant enough; and unwittingly did me a good turn, for without him I should never have known Den. "Are you going to Vancouver?" asked the conductor. " No, Salmon Arm. But I am stopping off at Golden for a couple of days on the way." Where's that you said?" " Salmon Arm." I enunciated more clearly this time. " It's just beyond " " Salmon Arm, did you say SALMON ARM?" A large young man shot at least a foot in the air from his seat opposite, took off his dark glasses, and leaned forward excitedly. " That's where I'm going!" " No. Are you really? Good Lord."

This, as I soon found out, was Den Meek. He was my "young giant" of this morning! He was a splendid figure of a man, at least six feet of him, with dark curling hair and a high forehead. Now that the sunglasses were at last off I could see he had deep-set, brown eyes – kindly, honest and penetrating eyes. An extraordinarily boyish smile had set them twinkling, lighting up his mature face.

I had never expected the name of my obscure destination to strike a chord in anybody's mind; neither, evidently, had he.

I do not know which of us was the most pleased. " It is my home town," said Den, " but I don't often meet anyone who has heard of it. I'm used to everyone saying, Salmon Arm, where the hell's that? " " So am I, but I never heard of it myself until a month ago

" It's God's own country. But how come you are going there? "

I tried, half apologetically, to explain the reasons for my impulsive journey, but Den understood at once.

" I wish I were you! " he exclaimed.

" That's exactly the kind of thing I want to do myself. " He looked dreamily out of the window for a moment, then turned to me almost fiercely. " I'm going to, too, one of these days," he said, and there was a new intensity in his voice; " only I want it to be somewhere really wild; somewhere where no men have ever been, where the trees and animals and birds live undisturbed and the pattern of nature is as it was meant to be. Where – but you don't want to hear about that." " Oh, but I do!"

" Tell me first, why did you pick on Salmon Arm?"

" The B.C. Government Travel Bureau sent me some folders of various places, and I fell in love with one photo on the Salmon Arm folder."

Mt. Ida from Gleneden near Salmon Arm, B.C.—6.   Donphoto.

The view that made me pick on Salmon Arm

" I didn't even know that Salmon Arm had a folder!" Den looked as pleased as if Salmon Arm was his own property. "Tell me, what was this particular photo?"

"Just a field, and a wooden fence, with trees and a mountain behind. But when I saw it I felt that if I could only work in that same field every day, and look up at that mountain, I should be perfectly happy. Silly, really."

" Not silly at all. Feelings are often more reliable than all the advice other people can give you.

I wonder if that was Mount Ida in the photo, what shape was it?"

"I'll show you. I've got the folder here in my writing-case."

We pored excitedly over the folder, and time passed unheeded until, in the late afternoon, the train came out onto the north shore of Lake Superior and we brought ourselves back to our present surroundings. We followed the shoreline for four hours. This was our first change of scenery, a short break in the monotony of that scrubby northern forest -short, but oh, how welcome!

I was glad I had made friends with Den, for in lovely places one needs someone to share one's feelings. He knew the place well but was not at all blase about it: he saw it with all the fresh wonder of a stranger, yet he could at the same time introduce it with the intimacy of an old friend. Best of all, he had the rare gift of silence: he told me just enough, then let the land speak for itself.

The shining waters of the Lake lay to our left, stretching away to a clear horizon which was broken only by small islands close in to the shore: it was hard to realize that this was all fresh water. Den told me that it could be as rough on the Great Lakes as on any sea; but that day there was scarcely a ripple, and the water shone white and steely grey under a cloudy sky. Lake and forest met and interlocked in a series of inlets and headlands, and the railway wound in and out along the jagged coastline thus formed, keeping faithfully to the water's edge. Time after time we would travel far inland up a narrow stretch of water, looking across at the long ridge of heavily timbered, rock- fringed land which was the next headland; then came a rattling and rumbling over a wooden trestle bridge, and suddenly we would find ourselves going once more towards the Lake, looking back across the water at our own tracks.

The land grew steeper and rockier, and for a few miles the train kept roaring through cuttings in the rock; every time we emerged, the changing views grew wilder and more exciting. The track curved so sharply that sometimes we could even see our own engine plunging into a tunnel, and the broken line of the train itself as it threaded its way in and out of the short deep cuttings.

It was a clear-cut landscape full of sharp contrasts. The islands and the mainland stood out steep and dark from the smooth, bright water, and the trees made a ragged line against the sky. The forest clothed the hills in a deep, living fur of green, as if to compensate for the harshness of the stony wastes and stark rocky shores; yet its rich greens joined with the warm red-brown of the rocks in defying the water's icy gleam Yes, icy: some of the inlets were full of ice and floating snow, although it was the end of May; and here and there a shrunken snowdrift still lay wearily across the rocks.

It was here that I saw my first booms – each a mass of huge floating logs, marshalled in orderly rows and held together by a single line of logs chained together around the outside. We did not leave the lake shore until after sunset, and before then I had supper with Den, and learned that he was a fully-fledged doctor. He had just finished his medical training in Toronto University, and was about to begin his first job in Vancouver. He was looking forward to it immensely. "I shall be in a hospital quite near U.B.C.," he said. "That's the University of British Columbia. I took my pre-med. there, so the old place is full of associations, and I still know some of the professors there."

I asked him when he would be beginning the job.

"Not till the middle of next week, but I shall only spend two nights a t home, as I have to find lodgings in Vancouver yet. Oh, but won't it ever be good to see home again, and Mother and Dad. I haven't been for two years."

I left him after supper, visited Janet in her first-class seat, and went back to bed, happy and very late, long after the mysterious curtains of Tourist Car No. 71 had formed a hushed green passageway. The young man from Calgary snored quietly in the berth over mine. I crawled into my housecoat and sat up, finishing the letter home:-

"We passed Fort William at 11:20 p.m., but put the clocks back one hour there. What a long day! "I have made friends with a very nice twenty-nine-year-old doctor who actually comes from Salmon Arm; he is visiting his parents there. He is all in the know and is going to help me, so I am cancelling the stop-over I was thinking of making at Golden, and going straight to Salmon Arm with him. He will introduce me to his father, who is the Bank Manager, and well known all around there, and can give me the right contacts. I think I must be born lucky!"

CHAPTER THREE

On the second morning, as before, I woke at dawn eager for fresh views. I knew we must be well into Manitoba by now, and I expected to have my first sight of the Prairies. I lay still a few minutes longer, relishing the anticipation. I remembered my old nursery geography book, in which the hero and his sister were taken on a magic carpet to Baghdad, the Pyramids, and all kinds of other interesting places; it was every bit as exciting, I reflected, to be rushing across Canada in a comfortable C.P.R. Berth! I had only to sit up in bed, and the dull old wheat-growing prairies prairies of the school text books would turn before my eyes to a vast and breathtaking reality. But when I did sit up I caught sight of that too familiar old line of tree tops, and sank back, disgusted. Still Ontario's forest! I remembered how, in England, the character of the countryside could alter may times during a few hours' drive, and marvelled afresh at the vastness of Canada. In two nights and a day, the four hours on the lake shore had been our only change of scenery.

At 9:14 a.m. We came into Winnipeg: poor, poor, Winnipeg. I had already heard much about the flood of the Red River there: the newspaper photographs had not exaggerated. Our train slowed down well before the city limits, and moved into the station at a snail's pace, and, safe on our high embankment, we stared down in horrified silence. The little wooden houses stood in a vast expanse of grey water. Only a rectangular pattern of wide, shining canals marked where the streets had been; and along the drowned avenues stood rows of patient trees, one-legged in the water like so may herons, each one guarding its reflection. Behind the houses, ridiculous clothes-lines were stretched over the water, while in front of them, an occasional wicket-gate thrust up a short row of little wooden points above the surface opposite a half submerged door; there was nothing else to show that there had been front gardens full of spring flowers, or back gardens waiting for the spring sowing of vegetables.

The train clanked on. From the iron railway-bridge we looked not down but along at the great swollen river: the water must have been very near the level of the train tracks. It stretched away dirty, cold, and relentless, to a line of buildings, where it reached high against the deserted walls and doors. It lapped greedily at the top of a long dyke of soggy-looking sandbags at the side of a road. The men who worked at reinforcing the sandbags might have been so many helpless grey ants, so pathetically were they trying to save their stricken city. If the Red River chose to go down now, the dyke would help prevent further damage; but if it rose a few more inches, well.... One could only pray.

I went to buy some sandwiches in the station (prices of meals in that Dining Car were prohibitive), and met Den in the Coffee Bar. He was having the most gigantic breakfast I had ever seen – coffee, cornflakes and cream, two plate-sized hotcakes swimming in syrup, and a mountain of buttered toast and marmalade. "It is the only way to do it," he said. "Have one real blow-out and make it last all day." He confessed to me that he "rather enjoyed being almost completely broke." "I like it better than just having some," he said. "It's fun to see how far a dollar can be stretched; and when one does buy something one appreciates it all the more for having waited for it."

Half an hour later we were steaming out of Winnipeg, away into the true Prairies. The Prairies held for me a strange and subtle joy, one which is hard to explain but which was very real and quite shattered my prejudices about flat land. But it took me some time to succumb to their spell. At first the countryside seemed unchanged: mildly undulating land, lifeless, wintry-looking cedar copses, some spruces, and here and there a gleaming pool of flood- water. The last straight rows of Winnipeg's suburban houses, white, wooden and bleak, gave way to isolated farms and occasional straggling villages. Too many trees, too many undulations: it did not seem to me to be at all what a Prairie should be.

Some time later, however, gazing absently out over the land, I suddenly realized that I must be looking at the Real Thing. Quite, quite flat, it was, just like that. Except that the undulations had vanished, it was much the same as before: there were green patches and brown patches, fences and straight dirt roads, farms standing in clusters of tree.

I was disappointed: I suppose I had expected to see a land devoid of trees or fences, a land in which each field would stretch, self-coloured, to the horizon. This was a land too varied, too much like places I had seen before. I stared at it disconsolately and tried to feel enthusiastic. I overheard scraps of other people's conversation, and the word "prairie" kept cropping up. This was undoubtedly the Real Thing. Prairied this, prairie that. I felt like the Toronto girls who had told me that I could "have the West." "The Manitobans can have their Prairie," I thought. "I don't want it!"

Then somebody asked me, "Well, what do you think of the Prairie?" "Not much," I said. The morning hours dragged by. I made myself wait until one o'clock before I ate my C.P.R. sandwiches, then as I ate I watched the countryside. It was still unchanged, although we must have covered over a hundred miles since leaving Winnipeg. Close to the tracks the grass and stones streaked by, merging into parallel lines of green and brown, while beyond them, slower, flowed the endless stream of trees and farms, long stretches of grass or bare soil, fence-posts, more farms, and trees again. Far beyond this backward-fleeing procession, the horizon slid past with infinite slowness, so slowly that I felt it was moving forward with the train, while all the land between would seem to turn slowly on itself, like a wheel with the train tracks tangent to the flying rim, and the hub just out of sight beyond the horizon.

The illusion was the same that I had had in English trains, only here the wheel of land was bigger, and even more hypnotic in its many-speeded spinning. I forced my eyes away from it to read another chapter of my book; but then they were drawn irresistibly back , and I sat there by the window watching, watching, watching...

Now I would watch the strange turning of the flat land under the steady following sky, waiting for fresh landmarks on the slow horizon, or letting myself get dizzy from the sight of the speed- blurred grass below the window. And now I would pick out the things that gave the landscape a character of its own: a wooden farmhouse clustered round with its wooden buildings and few scrawny trees; a dead-straight, muddy, unfenced road, parallel to the tracks, or running across them with a gate less level crossing; here, a line of gigantic grain elevators blocking out the entire view; and, over there, a few tiny ones on some branch track in the far, far distance. The farm houses must have been a long way apart, yet there were always plenty of them in my view; I imagined they were close together, and their farms between seemed disappointingly small.

Then all at once I began to realize the vastness of it all. This farm house by the track was full sized, but that one just behind it was in miniature, while the one a little further off was contracted to almost microscopic dimensions , as would be the very furthest houses you could pick out on a clear day from an English hill. Why, they were not close to each other at all! On this absolutely flat land even the most distant house stood up fearlessly on the horizon, silhouetted, with its attendant trees, against the sky, and looking for all the world as if it were only across the next field but one. Yet many of these houses, I calculated, must have been six or seven miles away – perhaps ten or even more.

I was looking out, not, as I had imagined, on a land of little farms and many houses, but on an enormous tract of countryside divided into comparatively few farms, and, to the English way of thinking, scarcely populated at all. It was all so vast that I had been unable to see its vastness. I gazed until the wonder began to wear off, but before the boredom returned, a fresh wonder broke over me in a great wave; the sky. Why, it was the greatest thing the Prairie had, its sky, and I had only just noticed it! The sky dominated the land, it covered it from end to end and from one side to another, with never so much as a hillock on the horizon to interrupt its full extending. The Prairie had more sky than any other place could boast, and, owning so much glory, had no need of mountains or of valleys.

The sky was not only greater here, it was different in itself. Instead of arching in the usual dome, it was hung like a great flat ceiling over this level floor of land. Crossed and re-crossed by bar after bar of cloud in parallel lines, this ceiling stretched away over the land in an infinity of perspective, never seeming to meet the horizon at all. I felt that I had discovered the secret of the Prairie, and next time I saw Den I shared the discovery with him. He had crossed Saskatchewan eight times before, but to him, too, this was a new and exciting aspect of the place; in that moment we were exploring together.

As most of the Prairie stations we explored together in other ways. "If you get out at the stations and go looking for it," Den assured me, "you can always find something interesting;" and he was right. At Regina we found a crate labelled "Calgary Zoo", and peering in through its cracks I saw my first opossums. At another station we watched chunks of fresh ice as big a chairs being loaded into the great tanks under the cars of our train. At Moose Jaw, after dark, Den went into the town and bought six bottles of beer which he smuggled with glee into the train – if such a procedure could be called smuggling. We were drawn aside at the station entrance by a railway official, but Den only squared his impressive shoulders, smiled his charming smile, and said: "Good evening."

"Good evening," said the official, stealing a quick glance at Den's bulging bag. For a minute they chatted like old friends, as strangers do in Canada. Then the official looked Den straight in the eye and dropped his voice. "You do know," he said slowly, "that it is illegal to bring any alcoholic drinks onto the train?" Den looked back at the official, also straight in the eye. "I do," he said.

The official drew down his solemnity more tightly over the escaping smile. "You realise that it is against the law?"

"I do," said Den, nodding gravely.

"You are quite clear about it?"

"Yes, yes, quite clear."

"Okay, so long as you know about it." The official grinned broadly, and we passed through, complete with beer.

We shared the beer with a party of University students in Den's car; everybody, including the coloured steward, waxed cheerful and sang every community song they could think of. At ten o'clock they all went to bed, but Den and I moved off to the Observation Car to talk. We spoke of Canada in general and British Columbia in particular; we discussed the relative merits of English and Canadian universities; and as the conversation passed on through science to religious education we became completely absorbed in it. One or two other people were reading there, but soon they went to bed, leaving only the conductor at one end of the car, and ourselves at the other.

Den began to tell me more about himself. "When I was at school," he said, "the last thing I wanted was to go on to University: my one idea was to get out into the bush. I figured on joining a logging camp, but Mother and Dad wouldn't hear of that, and they made me furious. We had some colossal arguments – my, I must have been an obnoxious kid! But Mother has the patience of an angel, and she persuaded me in the end that if I took some kind of training it would give me a chance to go on scientific expeditions into the bush. She's got some sense, has Mother. We fixed on the medical course. That appealed to me more than any other profession, and you see, they always want a doctor on these expeditions, and even if I couldn't manage to join one, I could be a doctor in a logging camp. That way I should still get a chance to study wild life on the side, and to take photographs.

"I did my pre-med years at U.B.C., then the war came and messed everything up, I was five years in the Air Force, but I came back and did the rest of the course at Toronto, and now here I am.

"My, I'm glad I listened to Mother: I love this work, and I wouldn't be doing any other for all the world. I like the chance of helping people; and I like the way the work never gets stale, there's always more to learn." I asked him if he still hoped to go with expeditions.

"Oh yes," he said. "Sure I do. After I have done two or three years in Vancouver I believe I have every chance of getting on something of the kind. It will help, too, being in touch with those U.B.C. Professors." "Which aspect of the 'wild life' is it that interests you so much?" I asked. "Birds, animals, or plants? Or just all of it?"

"All of it; but specially mammals. They fascinate me. I could talk to you for ages about them. When I was a kid I used to go up the mountain after dark and sit by a game-trail for hours on end, just watching. When you do that you have to keep absolutely still, hardly even blink: I used to get cold and stiff. But it was worth it, to see a fat, black bear shuffling along with his toes turned in, or a deer leaping, with great high leaps, over nothing at all. Or to hear the coyotes yapping: that's a sound you never forget. "When I got old enough Dad gave me a good camera, and I began taking flashlight photographs. I still do it whenever I get the chance . It may take hours and days, even weeks, to get a good animal picture, but it is most satisfying when you do. I have a few with me, I'll show them to you tomorrow, if you like.

At that moment two officials came in and asked us if we would like to go now, or be locked in till midnight: the Dining Car, which was between us and our beds, was to be cast off and replaced soon, meanwhile they were locking the doors at either end of it. We chose to stay till midnight.

We talked in the dim light while the conductor dozed in the far corner. Den told me of his home, of the city of Salmon Arm, of chipmunks and chickadees, fir trees and mountains, of quiet lakes and majestic valleys; and I fell still more deeply in love with the British Columbia of my dreams, the British Columbia which was so close to my heart but which I had not yet seen.

Creeping to bed very late and tiptoe quiet, and drifting to sleep for the third and last time in my little green bedroom, I was hardly conscious of my surroundings: for I could already smell the forest around me and feel the pine needles under my feet, and my heart was bursting with joy of the mountains seen between the trees. All night long the train roared on over the straight tracks, with the Prairie stretching away, dark and infinite, on either side.

CHAPTER FOUR

It was four o'clock when I woke up next morning. Grey trees, grey farmhouses, and grey grass were just beginning to separate themselves from the general blackness which was the Prairie.

I watched them slipping by until I grew tired of being propped up on one elbow, then dozed off again. An hour later I woke again, and the lightness in the sky had grown almost to the stature of daylight. Objects were no longer dim and mysterious, but all of the Prairie lay in hushed stillness, waiting for the sunlight to leap up over the horizon, warming it and dazzling it into life. Before the sunlight came the colours: spring greenness on the trees took the place of grey half-tones, and I saw patch after patch of some lovely yellow flower growing down on the bank beside the tracks. Oh dawn, spring, new lands! Oh, the mountains less than a day's journey off, and I to see them so soon! The joy of it almost hurt physically, I was so alive. I was alive enough for two, yet was still only one of me, and must keep quiet.

The bank below my window grew slightly higher, flattened down to nothing, and grew slowly again; but beyond it the land seemed even flatter, if that was possible, than that of yesterday. No more than a low bank raised itself occasionally, and still there was the same illusion of nearness, of smallness in a vast landscape.

For some time I half sat, half lay, staring at a long, low bank of yellow sand which lay, apparently, a few hundred yards away across the grass. Now and again I looked down at more white and yellow flowers below the window, but my eyes were always drawn back to this bank; I was sleepily interested in the sandy soil exposed there, for it was golden like sea sand. A band of dark trees hid it from view for a few minutes; then they were gone, and there was my sandbank, unchanged, and seeming to be no nearer. Odd, I thought, that it did not get any nearer, for it was ahead of the train: I had to twist myself round to in bed to see it at all.

Then in one stunning moment it happened: the sunlight caught up with us from behind and burst in full flood upon the world; while in the same moment from the west, ahead, the light came suddenly into my mind, and I realized what it was I was looking at the Rockies! My bank was no low bank, it was no less than a whole range of snowy peaks, the Rocky Mountains themselves, the land I longed for! What I had though to be golden sand was the gold of the morning sun, lighting up the high snow slopes and ice-clad rocks long before it rose upon the plains. And not a couple of hundred yards away, but miles! I looked at the timetable, looked at my watch, made a quick calculation: yes, about fifty they must be quite fifty miles from here. Fifty long miles ahead, yet the sunlit snow rose so high and clear against the sky. How tall to look thus far away, how huge they must be. How tall, and, oh, how full of majesty.

Mountains, real mountains at last. Mountains: my lovely dream word, now awake with meaning. Mountains: all the photographs, all the paintings treasured in the gallery of my memory fading into insignificance before this one unforgettable image now impressing itself upon me.

Mountains: the imagined mountains of books, of conversations, of other people's anecdotes, becoming nothing in face of the mountains of my own personal, now-at-this-moment, very first experience. The knowledge had been a lovely thing, but the actual realization was infinitely better!

I needed to shout, to sing, to dance. I needed everybody to share this thing with me. Mountains, mountains! I longed to run up and down the car flinging back everybody's curtains, shouting to them: "Wake up! Look! The Rockies, you can see the Rockies! See, come and look what I have seen! Over there, oh look, the Rocky Mountains!"

That was what I wanted, what I needed to do, but one does not do these things. Everyone must go on sleeping, stuffily sleeping, and with their blinds drawn down, too, most of them. I had to let them sleep, let them miss this miracle.

Calgary. At eight o'clock in the morning, Calgary, where the Prairie ends and the foothills begin. Ranching country all around, land of cowboys and cow-ponies, land of rodeos, of white-faced cattle, of horses running wild upon the hills. Calgary, the home of my dark and handsome travelling companion with the Stetson hat. Calgary, first city in the land where they wear bluejeans and ten-gallon hats, and ride in high Western saddles. Here they hold the famous Stampede every year, and people pour in from all over the Dominion to watch the rodeos and the perilous chuck-wagon races teams of four galloping full tilt through the mud with the great four- wheeled covered wagons hurtling after them. How I longed to come and watch on the great day only another month or so to go! That was probably out of the question; but anyway, here I was, if only for half an hour, at Calgary, the entrance to the West at last.

As soon as the train stopped I went out into the town. I crossed the road and went straight on, leaving the station directly behind me. Ahead, the street went uphill a little, and vanished in a curve. It was good to see a street that was neither level nor dead straight; and even better to see the hills rising up beyond it, wild and bare, and looking so near. The country felt very close on all sides, and the whole city seemed to me to be clean and full of fresh air, and wonderfully lacking in factories. And all the time I could sense the nearness of the Rockies, although here the great range was hidden by its foothills. If I had to live in a city, I thought, I would not mind living here, with those hills at the end of every street, and Banff only a few hours away, and the Stampede every year.

After Calgary I kept my nose glued to the window, for outside the country was no longer flat, neither was it monotonous with birch and jack-pine forest. This was a land of gentle, sweeping hills, wide and wild and bare. Only a very few scrubby trees, hardly ever a fence, and often a high bare rocky patch. A dry country: we never passed a lake, and I could not catch sight of any streams; yet it was green then, for May is the green time of year. And oh, it was big! Acres and acres of green slopes, broad dales, and stony hilltops, with sometimes only a lonely group of houses in the entire landscape, sometimes no sign of human habitation at all for miles.

Scatterings of red dots which were the Hereford cattle grazing, and occasionally a herd of shining horses, beautiful with their rippling muscles, flowing manes and tails, and their many different colours. Fine horses they were, and as free and wild as the Exmoor ponies at home. I was too excited to speak. Den was watching too, and we exchanged glances and gazed again, until the horses were out of sight. Once we passed a casual, blue-jeaned rider on a chestnut horse, sauntering down a path and waiting by a gate to cross the railway. He was almost close enough to touch, and I gazed like a fascinated child, for this was the very first time I had seen the Western style of riding in real life.

Now and again we saw more horses, and cattle; but mostly the country was empty of life, a lonely sea of solid Normanows, tumbling and lifting, green and grey and brown, sweeping away and away on either side, mile after mile.

Gradually the hills became wilder and steeper, and the stony patches changed to crags. The trees began again, and here and there a tall peak towered between them. I held my breath. It was gone; but here came another; and here, almost on top of us, crowned with overhanging rocks and streaked with snow which shone against the sky, a mountain , a real, true mountain!

"Oh, Den, look!"

Suddenly there seemed to be mountains everywhere. We were here at last, and I could not take it in quickly enough. I did not know whether to laugh or cry.

"Oh, Den!"

But Den had been here before. "You save your excitement up for the real mountains later on," he said. "These aren't mountains, these are only foothills. You wait till you see the real Rockies, after Banff."

So these were only foothills. What rubbish! Why, here came one that could only be seen be twisting one's neck and looking upwards, face pressed against the window!

Every minute they became more impressive, but I tried to be calm and pretend that they were not mountains at all. Den said quietly, "Look over there – elk." I followed his gaze, and sure enough, there they were, two great, brown deer-like creatures moving among the trees; and another, and another, only a few yards from the tracks, and not at all disturbed by the train.

Then there was nothing but trees, with a cleared strip ten yards wide on either side of the tracks; and on the cleared strip, far too often, was a dead horse – a new sight to me. A little later I realized that we actually were among mountains at last; even Den admitted it. He said we were now within Banff National Park.

Near Banff

At Banff we got out for a few minutes and wandered up and down by the train.

The sun poured down on the little station with its long platform of parched concrete, and the air was clear, fresh, mountain air, heady like a draught of wine. I wished I had not packed my camera at the bottom of my biggest case, for the mountains were magnificent all around: great proud shapes reared up against the sky, unbelievably high up, their white snows broken with parallel lines of rugged strata. Below those wild, craggy rocks the snow lay virginal on the steep slopes; lower down it became speckled with trees, until it was lapped in a sea of dark fir forest which stretched, swollen with wooded hills, from the feet of the furthest mountains to the outskirts of the town.

"I've ridden all over there," said Den casually indicating the vast landscape to the south. "At least, over a good deal of it."

"You've ridden here?"

"Sure!" Den laughed. "I came up here for one of the summer vacations when I was at U.B.C., and worked as a guide on the trail-rides. Best job I ever had, that."

I looked at him with new respect, and not a little envy.

Gliding away from Banff, we caught sight of the famous Banff Springs Hotel away to the south. It is a huge, expensive, modern palace, isolated in an incredibly beautiful setting high among the fir-clad hills. The green forests rise behind it into the rocks and snows of Sulphur Mountain and Mount Rundle, and fall away in front of it, to reach out to the feet of the far peaks in the east and west, and to the town and railway below the wall of mountains in the north. It must be a wonderful place to stay at.

A wonderful place, that is, if one wants to be a tourist. But I did not want to be a tourist. I did not want to dine to fine orchestral music in famous dining-rooms, as the advertisements invited me to do, nor to dance in spacious ballrooms; I did not want the golf, tennis, swimming, or even the trail-riding; nor did I want the glory of being able to say afterwards: "I stayed at Banff – oh, yes, the Hotel, of course - and at Lake Louise; the scenery was just out of this world, my dear." No, what I was after was an inner knowledge of the country itself" I wanted to know the forest trails, the local birds and flowers, some small quiet lake, one or two villages; to know, above all, what it felt like to be someone who lived in British Columbia, and afterwards to be able to say, "Why, sure I've seen chipmunks, I worked on a farm in B.C. for two months, one summer."

We left Banff behind, and continued along an ice-green river between rows of towering peaks. The mountains were so beautiful, so wild, so supremely aloof and indifferent to mankind, that I put away my C.P.R. guidebook with its sketch-maps. The peaks in their beauty spoke for themselves, one did not need to know their names and heights. I pressed against the window, eager to absorb every bit of this fantastic parade of proud pinnacles, afraid to miss one jagged line of fir-tree tops, one gleaming snow slope, or one overhanging rock.

"Somewhere along here," said Den, "are the beaver dams, just after Mount Eisenhower. Now, they're round this next bend, I think. Should be about here, any minute now... Oh, no, not here must be the next bend... Ah, here we are! Just coming up. There! See?"

We stared, fascinated, and strained our eyes for a sight of a beaver. The railway runs close past one of the meanderings of the Bow River in its wide valley, and there the beavers have chosen to live. As we went past we saw their artificial pond, which must have been at least two acres in size. All across the far end stretched a most efficient looking dam of close-knit logs and branches; and over a wide area on either side of the river most of the trees had been felled.

I longed to see one of the little animals that worked so hard and were such expert engineers, but there was no sign of life on the shining water, nor among the brushwood on the banks. As we crossed the river and plunged once more into the fir trees, the beaver pond was hidden from view. A minute later we saw it again through a clearing, gleaming far off among the trees, then it was gone for good. No beavers. I was sorry to have missed them; but I knew I should always remember seeing their work.

We steamed on up the valley, past peaks nine, ten, and eleven thousand feet high; then we crossed the river and climbed into a narrower valley. Somebody told me to look out for the Great Divide. This is the division not only between two provinces, but also of a small stream into two yet smaller branches. It is a more significant division than it would at first appear; for, of the two little brooks, one flows back eastward to join the Bow River, bound eventually for Hudson's Bay and the Atlantic; while the other runs westward into the Columbia and thus to the Pacific.

The Divide is marked by an archway of timber, with small logs nailed in the shapes of letters across the top to spell the words THE GREAT DIVIDE; on the left, also written in thin logs, is ALBERTA, and on the right, BRITISH COLUMBIA. I glowed inside; British Columbia at last!

British Columbia at last (The Great Divide)

A moment later we were at the entrance to the Kicking Horse Pass. "And now," said Den, his dark eyes gleaming, "comes the most exciting part of all."

A seething white river plunged alongside us as we went down the canyon-like pass. The mountains closed in like great stern prison walls high above us on either side, and the stiff spires of the trees stood motionless, pointing darkly to the sky. Nothing moved but the train and the foaming river beside it, both racing madly as if to escape the cold, blind gaze of the watching mountains.

Suddenly the narrow pass came to an end, and our view opened up. We were perched high up on the mountainside, with the land dropping away down on our right, down, down to a big, curving river. The valley was full of pointed trees and tumbled rocks, and from it the cliffs and screes rose up and up, tier upon tier, forming three massive mountains, one opposite us, one half behind us, and the one we were on – Cathedral Mountain. The lower slopes of these three overlapped each other, hiding from view all but half a mile or so of the river. Ahead of us were vertical cliffs, buttressed with huge crags and steeply roofed with a rising tumult of rock and snow architecture in excelsis, how right that they should be called Cathedral Crags!

"Now for the Spiral Tunnels!" exclaimed Den, drawing his chair even closer to the window. He had explained them thoroughly to me in advance, and was now making sure I missed nothing. Although I knew, in a sense, exactly what to expect, now I was here I found it all quite overwhelming.

Down on our right, Den showed me where we would be in a few minutes' time – tracks running parallel to the ones we were on, some fifty feet further down the mountainside.

"But we'll be going back that away," he said, pointing in the direction we had come from.

Before I had taken this in, he beckoned me back to the left windows and pointed ahead and upwards at Cathedral Crags. "See the old mine there?" "No, higher up." And I saw it, a round black hole, a mere speck on the face of the rock wall, so high that it made me feel sick to think of the men who had gone in and out of it, working there every day. "See the ice?" he asked quietly. I looked higher, and again even higher, almost overhead; and my unaccustomed eyes were opened and I saw that a green smoothness at the cliff-top was ice, thick curtains of green ice hanging there, rippled, sea-green ice and merging icicles. The strangeness and the beauty grew nearly unbearable; then, whoom! it was gone. Gone, and only a blackness left, and our own reflections in the window.

We were in the tunnel long enough for me to realize that we were inside Cathedral Mountain, as much as that old mine-shaft was inside it; long enough to get used to the dim lights; and long enough to try, in vain , to feel as if the train was turning in a circle. Then all at once we were out again, blinking in the daylight, and the pit of the valley was on the wrong side, on our left. Ahead we could see both the entrance and the exit of the next tunnel, and the way the railway curved off left to reach them. After a moment we could see, too, the position of the higher track up above us, where we had just been.

Upper Spiral Tunnels   Field

As we curved round I saw the Crags again from further off: the whole Titanic cathedral wall, with its snow, its rocky buttresses, and the sheer cliff tipped with blue- green ice. Then I was looking down at more railway tracks coming out directly beneath us, at right angles to our present path; and a moment later, whoom! it was dark again, and we were in the second tunnel. When we came out, the valley had righted itself and we were travelling west again, down by the green and foam-flecked waters of the Kicking Horse River. A few miles further on we stopped at Field, and Den and I got out to stretch our legs again and admire the mountains. They were spectacular but very bare and rocky, and overpoweringly close: I felt shut in and afraid. Stale smoke from the trains hung in the air at the valley bottom, and smelt horrible. I learned that it was here that the eastbound trains stopped and had extra engines put on to haul them up the next few miles, through the Spiral Tunnels and up the Kicking Horse Pass to Stephen. Placed at intervals along the platform were odd little signposts, barely two feet high, pointing up at crazy angles to the various peaks. I read the names and altitudes written on them, especially the altitudes, which all seemed to run into five figures: 10,495; 11,686; my brain reeled.

At field we had to put our watches back another hour, changing from Mountain to Pacific Time, and the afternoon seemed to stretch ahead of us for ever.

Lower Spiral Tunnels   Field

CHAPTER FIVE

It was as unforgettable afternoon, almost too long to bear, yet far too short for seeing so much beauty. Hour after hour we sped on down valleys and canyons, always exchanging one splendid view for the next, too quickly, far too quickly. It was as if one were looking at a book of beautiful pictures and somebody kept turning the pages over before one had looked long enough. We rushed past open views up branch valleys, showing distant snow-capped peaks; under steep screes and overhanging cliffs; and over deep gorges full of the roaring of torrents in their depths. Here and there we passed a patch of graceful poplars, and everywhere the tall spikes of the lodge-pole pines softened the mountain slopes with a fur of green tips, from the timber line down to the river banks, where their close ranks stopped short, showing a naked cross-section, a row of close, straight trunks like the teeth of a fine comb.

Kicking Horse Canyon

All these things I watched with Den; and he told me all I most wanted to know about the mountains, trees, birds and flowers that we saw, but – to my unending gratitude – none of those boring, guidebook statistics which would have clogged first impressions. He knew how to be silent before beauty. Once he murmured, half to himself: "There's so darn much in life that is lovely, it beats me why more people don't see it."

In the end he went back to his own seat and persuaded me to go to mine.

"You ought to relax for a bit," he said. "Stop trying to take it all in; you can't do it, it's too much. I'm going to have a sleep for an hour or so, and I should do the same if I were you."

But sleep was out of the question. I did try shutting my eyes once or twice, but I couldn't help opening them after two or three minutes: I couldn't bear to miss anything! We were high on the side of a narrow valley, climbing into the Selkirk Mountains. Now and again the train rattled over perilously high truss bridges, crossing the gorges of mountain creeks which hurtled down to join the river far below. I peered down at each white ribbon of water, holding my breath until we were safely off each bridge; but now I had to keep all my excitements to myself.

Once, we went into a long tunnel, and I closed my eyes and relaxed for a few minutes, for the first time since leaving Calgary. I tried to think of nothing, and found my brain full of the lilting name of our next river: "Illecillewaet, Illecillewaet, Illecillewaet....." I had no idea how to pronounce it, but I knew it must sound lovely anyway.

When we burst out into daylight again the view was more splendid than any we had yet seen. Close around us were glaciers and precipices; in the distance, a magnificent panorama of peaks; and, below and ahead of us, the river with the lovely name, winding its way down a great valley too lovely for any name, lovelier than a poem. Down its full length of forty miles we followed this valley, tearing through woods and canyons, under tunnels and snow-sheds, past creeks and side valleys and towering peaks, racing the river in its mad rush to join the Columbia.

At last we came to Revelstoke, almost in the Salmon Arm area. The train stopped there for twenty minutes, and I got out for fresh air and a look around. The station nestles under Mount Revelstoke, at the foot of the southern slopes; and when we came there everything was drenched in the warm gold light of the evening sun. I fell in love with the place at once. Den's deep voice hailed me from behind, I waited for him and we wandered about together. It was good to share things with him again. I remember big, shady trees, a bank of garden flowers, and, most wonderful of all, my first wild tulips. I had hardly taken Den seriously when he had told me that in British Columbia the tulips grew wild in the grass; but here they were, small but brilliant cups, growing on long, slender stalks among all the uncut grass. I found them so perfect, so touching, and so astonishing, that I quite forgot to notice the view. I could think only of the tulips, of the grass sloping up to the trees, of the snowy heights of Mount Revelstoke out of sight up yonder, and, somewhere between those trees and the summit, of the Alpine meadows Den described, full of all kinds of mountain flowers. It was the first place I had wanted to stop at, to explore thoroughly: I was getting near home!

It was a quarter past six when we slid out of Revelstoke on the last lap of the journey. With the great barriers of the

Rockies and the Selkirks now behind us, we went through the more gentle Monashee Mountains by valleys full of huge trees and lush undergrowth, with wild foaming rivers roaring down them. We went through rocky canyons hung with giant ferns; and once the train threaded its way in and out of little tunnels along the steep shore of a lake full of the deep green shimmering of reflected forests.

Den came to sit with me, and I introduced him to my latest travelling companion, Mrs. Hope. Mrs. Hope came from Toronto, and was on her way to her son's wedding at Sicamous, two stations before Salmon Arm. She was one of the most charming people I had ever met. She was very impressed with my "Great Western Adventure", and made me promise to write and let her know how I got on, pressing me with invitations to come and see her if I should return to Toronto.

"I'd very much like to see you again and hear all about it," she said, "and yet I hope you won't be back in Toronto; I can see how much you love the West. I hope you will meet some nice young man and make your home out here."

Mrs. Hope was genuinely surprised when I told her I was twenty-six. "She still has that look of wonder in her eyes," she said to Den, who agreed. I felt that nobody could see the Rockies for the first time, and come through the Selkirks and down through the Monashees into the heart of British Columbia, without a look of wonder coming into their eyes.

Gradually the undergrowth became more lush, and the valley widened out; soon we were passing small farms with pocket-handkerchief fields hard-won from the tenacious "bush". The mountains were hardly more than big hills:

still streaked with snow on top, still bearing proud crags and rocky cliffs, but now all below the timber-line. Spruce and cedar, pine and hemlock fuzzed up every slanting skyline, climbing over the very summits, scattering sparsely among rocks, sprouting bravely out of the face of some precipice, or crowding densely to make the rich, green velvet pile of a mountain's cloak.

It was nearly dark when we came at last to Sicamous, where the journey's last river emptied itself into Shuswap Lake.

Before I said goodbye to Mrs. Hope, she insisted on introducing me to her mother, who had come up from Vancouver to meet her. "Mother is English," she had said. "When we get to Sicamous you must meet her: I know she'd love to see you, specially as you're just out from the Old Country."

Sure enough, the little old lady did seem genuinely pleased to meet me; and, although we were only together for a couple of minutes, she gave me her address and begged me to come and see her if ever I should go to Vancouver. I was deeply touched; I stood gazing after mother and daughter as they walked off down the platform, and marvelled at the friendliness and hospitality of the Canadian people. Canadians by birth and Canadians by choice, they all seemed to be like this.

Den, who had been back to his own seat to get his luggage together, came and joined me again.

"That was one very, very, charming woman," he remarked.

I nodded. "The old mother was a dear, too. Aren't people nice?"

"Mm."

We went to the edge of the platform and looked out over the lake, leaning on a rail. Dark, wooded mountains stood hushed on every side, their pine-serrated outlines rounded against the sky, steeply dropping to the shores, and thrusting low, tree-spiked, black headlands out across the silver water.

Shuswap Lake, my lake at last! I had dreamed of just such a mountain lake; a lake to shine below the fields where I worked, a lake to sail on, to bathe in, to sit beside; and all around it the freedom of the untamed bush, spreading over mountain and valley and mountain again, boundless.... I had found my lake on the map, and learned its shape; I had seen it in photographs and learned a little of its character; and finally I had met Den who had been brought up beside it, and who spoke of it intimately, lovingly. I knew it already so well in my heart; and now, now I had at last come to its shore, I looked on it and loved it at once. A great calmness came upon me, and the day's exhaustion was smoothed away.

Beside me, Den looked on the lake and loved it too, and we had no need of words. And, because for a little space there was no past and no future, the moment became one of those lovely things which never die in the memory, which make hardships easier to bear, and which no one can ever take away.

Only once Den spoke, and then almost in a whisper: "What I love is the way it is so quiet, so absolutely quiet."

A motor boat chugged busily by the wharf, the water slap-slapped against the shore below us, and everywhere the night air was full of the song of frogs. I smiled to myself: but then I saw that these things only underlined the stillness of the mountains and the water, they made a quietness, a peace, more deep than utter silence.

When the train moved on again, Den and I stood together in the little lobby place between the outside doors, at the end of Tourist Car No. 71, and continued watching the lake. The gleaming water grew wider; and, as we moved, slowly the dark curtains of hill and headland on our right withdrew, until we could see a great stretch of the lake reaching far away to the north, a flood of silver in an ebony valley. Then, from the left, a silhouetted headland slid out across the silver, and silently, inevitably, drew its mountain curtain across the scene. Now we were following the long western arm of the lake, at the end of which lay Salmon Arm. We traced the line of the shore, curving this way and that, and roaring through rocky cuttings on the steeper headlands. In and out we went, and on and on; while a mile away on the opposite shore the deep woods ran down to rocky cliffs and sandy beaches, sharp points and shallow bays; and in between the water lay, deep and still and quiet, scarcely ever varying in width.

Den reminisced about boat trips and boyhood camps, showing me the beaches where he had picnicked; and I became so infected with his love of home and joy in returning, that I felt the excitement of homecoming even more intensely than I used to feel it when going back to North Devon from school, to a life of hills and sea and searching-for-curlew's-nests-before-breakfast with big brothers. I knew the plants and animals, farms and cities, mountains and moods of this district; I knew the shape of the lake and the geographical position of everything; but, for the present, I had completely forgotten how I had come by this knowledge. So, when round every corner things were where I had expected them to be, and looked as I had expected them to look, I felt almost as though I had been here before – most certainly as though Fate had always intended that I should come here. Every mountain, every village, every curve of the lake shore, held for me the double magic of newness and familiarity, the stimulation of first encounter bound up with the relief of reunion. It was all immensely satisfying.

Salmon Arm B.C. Arrived May 25th 1950.

We had only one more stop before Salmon Arm: a brief halt at Canoe, which was the only inhabited place on all the twenty miles of shore between Sicamous and Salmon Arm. I watched the little row of lights by the track, and the few scattered ones up on the hillside; I saw the large pile of sawdust which indicated the presence of a sawmill, and the steep and lonely valley rising up behind; and I wondered what kind of people lived in such a place. Then even in those few moments, I grew impatient with the delay, and was glad when we moved on again.

Only fifteen minutes more! Den and I had to part company to collect our respective belongings, but he made me promise to wait for him on the platform and be introduced to his parents. They would help me fix up something for the night, he said, and if nothing could be found at a hotel, well, he was sure Mother would manage to put me up somehow. Both his parents were English and he was very anxious I should meet them, and sure that they would help me settle and find my job. I wondered nervously how they would feel about me, and what they would be like; but I was very grateful there was going to be somebody in Salmon Arm who might be my friend right from the beginning.

The coloured steward helped me bring my cases out into the little lobby, and stood with me while I watched the lights of Salmon Arm come into view in exactly the right place, inevitably yet incredibly. He was kind and friendly, and I confided to him some of my plans, some of my excitement. When at last he helped me down the steps I was really sorry to say goodbye to him: for, as he climbed back into the train, I felt none of the thrill of arriving, but only the cold loneliness of parting. It hurt to leave these new friends, and to leave my little green bedroom and all the other familiar comforts of the train which had been a kind of home to me for the past three days; and, most of all, it hurt to come down to earth, to wake from the fantasy of travelling into the hard reality of being in one place.

I shivered in the cold night air, and it occurred to me that, although the train had arrived on schedule at 8:30 p.m., in Salmon Arm it would now be 9:30 p.m., Pacific Summer, or rather "Daylight" Time. I put my watch forward accordingly. I had forgotten that the railways stuck to Standard Time. 9:30 p.m. is a bleak hour to arrive at a small strange town at the far end of a strange continent, especially when one has made no arrangements whatever, and is dog-tired into the bargain. I picked up the two suitcases which were all I had brought out West with me, and found them very heavy. I staggered off down the long platform towards the station buildings, wondering what on earth I was going to do next. Den was nowhere to be seen, and it seemed wrong to go and look for him and barge into a family reunion. Perhaps I should slip away on my own? I put the cases down and picked them up again, hesitant, suddenly panicky.

Then Den appeared from nowhere, took the cases, and bore me off before I had time to decide anything. I found myself shaking hands with his parents: in the dim light all I noticed was that Mrs. Meek was small and brisk in manner, while her husband was tall and slow. Then I was being helped into a black car with red tartan coverings on the seats. The "trunk" at the back was already crammed with Den's own belongings, so he pushed my luggage in onto the floor and the seat beside me and climbed in after it. An earnest discussion immediately began, as to which of the two hotels they should try first. Everybody was quite definite about one thing, that I should not be lost sight of until I was safely installed somewhere; and in less than two minutes I found myself alone in the car with Mrs. Meek, while Den and his father inquired at the first hotel. She seemed kind enough, but I was very nervous about what she would think of the whole situation. I tried to thank her for all this unwonted help, but she brushed my thanks aside and asked me polite questions about my plans.

Soon the two men came back across the road and said it was all okay, they had fixed a room for me. Den carried my cases in for me, and he and his father both came and waited while I signed the register, making quite sure I really was safely fixed up for the night. Everybody said goodnight and wished me luck, Den promised to ring me next day, and they drove off into the darkness.

I went straight to bed, and slept like a log.

CHAPTER SIX

CAPABLE ENGLISH GIRL, recent immigrant to Canada, seeks employment on mixed farm May – August. Experienced horses and dairy. Write to Box 1777, Observer. Three weeks before, I had sent the advertisement to the Salmon Arm Observer, together with two dollars and a letter explaining that I wanted it inserted for three consecutive weeks, but that I should like the replies saved up for me until my arrival during the third week.

On that first morning in Salmon Arm I could hardly wait to know the results. I tried to be prepared for the worst, for so many people had told me how unlikely it was that I would find the job that I wanted; all these small farms, they had said, were run by families who could not afford outside help. But I did hope and hope there would be replies waiting for me; just one reply – even an unsuitable one – would be something.

Having woken early, and being too excited to sleep again, I unpacked and pottered about in my room. After three months of sleeping on the couch in my sister's sitting-room, folding the bedclothes away every morning, I appreciated having a whole bedroom to myself. It was a drab little room, the lock on the door would not work, and the washing arrangements consisted of a jug and basin on a table in the corner; but I enjoyed spreading myself; and there was a big window overlooking a tidy garden with lawns and shady evergreen trees.

After breakfast I went out of the front door and down the broad shallow steps outside, and found myself in what was apparently the main street. I crossed this and took the first turning up an unpaved road to the right. The sun blazed down on the white sidewalks and on the bleached dust of the road, and I was glad of my dark glasses. I went uphill past a garage, a cafe, and a bicycle shop; then suddenly I saw the sign OBSERVER OFFICE straight ahead. It had taken less than two minutes to find it.

I ran up the hill as if my life depended on it, so that when I got there I had to waste precious time outside the door, getting my breathe back. I looked at the few photographs in the window, and especially at a copy of the familiar Salmon Arm folder. Now then! I took a deep breath and grasped the door handle.

Locked. Nobody in. I was furious, and rattled the handle. Somebody came by and told me kindly that the office would not be open until ten. I swore inwardly, then went over to the Post Office opposite to inquire for mail; but there was nothing for me yet.

So I went exploring. I went back into the main street, Alexander Avenue, past my hotel, and out onto Front Street. The names of the streets were written along the kerb stones at every corner. Front Street and Alexander Avenue seemed to be the only metalled roads in the place. Everything stopped short at Front Street: it corresponded to the front at a seaside resort, only in place of the sea there was the railway running across, with a line of poplar trees beyond it, then low, flat marshy fields, and finally the gleam of Shuswap Lake. Between Front Street and the railway there was an enormous parking-space, almost empty, with the station offices at one end and a big warehouse at the other. Opposite the end of Alexander Avenue, a huge notice-board stood in front of the parking-lot, bidding everybody "Welcome to Salmon Arm, the Jewel of the Shuswap Valley."

Front street - just outside Margery's office

At ten o'clock I went back to the newspaper office, and found it open this time. The editor himself came to the counter and introduced himself as Jack Howard. When I explained who I was, he beamed all over his face and went straight to a shelf and fetched a small sheaf of papers.

"You mean I've got a reply?"

Mr. Howard did not speak, but his eyes twinkled as he laid the papers in front of me. He leaned on his elbows on the counter and became very businesslike, very confidential.

He picked up a slip of paper on which were scribbled a telephone number and some notes in pencil "Now, this one wants you to ring her up." He read the notes aloud. "It seems just domestic, not farming at all, I shouldn't think that would suit you."

I looked it over and agreed with him.

Then he handed me a letter addressed to Box 1777. There was also a message pencilled on the outside of my own envelope, in which I had sent the original advertisement. Three replies! It was almost too good to be true.

I opened the letter and tried to concentrate on it. It was from a Mrs. Madrowski, whose husband was a colonel. They had two small children and a resident governess, and wanted me to work as land girl. I gathered it would be chiefly dairy and garden work. It certainly seemed more attractive that the domestic job, and I liked the sound of Mrs. Madrowski from her letter: friendly, frank, and businesslike; and she said she was English.

Mr. Howard was ready to tell me more about the Madrowskis. Col. Madrowski, he informed me, was a Polish Count. Although Mr. Howard did not actually say anything against him, and although he confessed he did not know the Madrowskis at all, he seemed very suspicious of the Polish Count's character. He went on to tell me, however, that the Madrowskis lived somewhere out beyond Tappen, a village ten miles away along the lake shore, and that Mrs. Madrowski usually came into Salmon Arm in the car on Mondays and Thursdays. A pity today was a Friday; but he could probably arrange a lift out there for me, if I wanted to go and look in a hurry.

Mr. Howard shook his head over the Madrowski job, and, for no very clear reason, seemed to think it would not do for me. The one he really was keen on was the third reply, which consisted of a note on my envelope: "P.B. Herald, calling in Thursday." "Now the Heralds," he said warmly, "I know you'd like them: they really are lovely people. I know them quite well - at least, I know the son and daughter, they come into town every week, and I usually see them. There's the four of them over there; the old Doctor and wife...."

Mr. Howard launched into an enthusiastic description of an extraordinary but apparently delightful family who lived across the lake; a moving tale of their desperate need for help and perennial difficulty in getting it; and a direct appeal to me to help them. But he put me off by his anxiety and enthusiasm: I had thought he was being wonderfully helpful to me, but now I realized I was coming in useful in his helpfulness to another client. The Heralds did sound charming, indeed; but all rather too old for me (even the two "children" were over forty), and definitely far too isolated. Not what I wanted, at all. In any case, there was no possibility of contacting them until Monday, and then only by ringing a store in Canoe on the off-chance that the son or daughter might be shopping there. They would not be in Salmon Arm until next Thursday.

I said I would think about it. I would concentrate, for the present, on the Madrowski job. Mr. Howard said he knew a Mrs. MacDonald who lived in Tappen and was in Salmon Arm today: he was sure she would give me a lift, and he would tele- phone me at the hotel in the afternoon and let me know.

I spent the rest of the morning in and out of Mr. Howard's office. He was most helpful and interested. He introduced me to his plump and cheerful wife, and told me all about his job and how interesting it was, especially as he tried to do so much more than his job. He appeared to know almost everybody in the district, and all their doings, although he had only been there for a few months. Before that he had been down on the Coast as a reporter on one of the big Vancouver papers.

Nothing was too much trouble. He even got hold of a girl who had once lived in Birmingham, and introduced us because we were both "from the Old Country."

Things certainly seemed to be going easily for me. I felt even more warmly towards Salmon Arm, and explored the town in between visits to Mr. Howard. It was what the Canadians call a "city", because its population was over 500; but it was only the size of a large English village. There were plenty of shops, or "stores", as I was learning to call them; also there were plenty of cafes, a cinema, a shipping office, two or three garages, and innumerable estate agents' offices. Beyond the shops the roads and lanes trailed off, straight and white and dusty, lined with wide grass verges and white wooden houses in unfenced gardens, away towards the green forested slopes of the mountains. The scene was dominated by Mount Ida, already an old friend of mine through the photograph in the folder. Everywhere the ground was bone dry, and the midday summer sun blazed down.

I rang up the lady who wanted domestic help, and refused her politely. Then I had lunch out at a snack bar, and spent the afternoon ironing my dresses in the hotel kitchen, poring over Mrs. Madrowski's letter in my bedroom, and wondering about the eccentric Heralds.

At about half past four Mr. Howard rang me up and said he had seen Mrs. MacDonald, who had agreed to take me out to Madrowski's farm that evening. Could I be ready at his office at quarter to six? He would himself telephone the Madrowskis and tell them about the arrangement. I said that would be fine, and thanked him very much.

Privately, I hoped that the visit would not take too long, as I did not want to miss Den's promised telephone call. I did tell the hotel proprietor – a doddering old man – that I was expecting a call, and he did promise to take a message and let me know as soon as I got back; but I had grave misgivings about his memory.

CHAPTER SEVEN

Mrs. MacDonald, a well-dressed, middle-aged woman, was waiting in her car when I got up to the Observer office. She drove off as soon as Mr. Howard had introduced us, and took me right to the farm. We had to go north along the lake shore to Tappen, ten miles from Salmon Arm, and then up a narrow and bumpy lane for another three miles. We drove up and up, round corners and under tall woods, with the Lake shining far behind and below us. We were surrounded by little hills; and the great bulk of Tappen Mountain and Spruce Hills towered over everything, so near yet never seeming any nearer for all our driving. Then suddenly we came out into more open country, into a most exclusive and special valley, a surprise valley.

One broad, sweeping curve it was, carpeted with rich green fields and bounded by the high mountains. On the left rose Tappen Mountain itself, free here from its clutter of scrubby foothills; its steep sides were thick with timber right down to the edges of the fields, and at the top its bare, red crags pushed fiercely out between the trees. On the right rose another ridge – lower, but with the same red crags, and the same wild, steep forest cascading down to the farmlands.

It was under this smaller ridge that the Madrowskis' farm nestled, looking out across its own broad fields to a similar farm on the other side of the valley. No other dwelling was in sight; only the two farms, the gentle green slopes, the steep, thick forest with its great red rocks, and the hot sunshine drenching everything.

Mrs. MacDonald herself lived at the opposite farm. She told me a certain amount about my possible employers, and though she was discreet, I did not like the way she kept speaking of displaced persons. All Col. Madrowski's former farm workers seemed to have been D.P.'s, and perhaps he would take me for one and treat me as such.

Here we were, at the farm itself. I jumped out to open the gate, and while Mrs. MacDonald drove through and came to a halt under some pine-trees I steeled myself to meet my fierce Polish Count and his English wife.

Almost at once Mrs. Madrowski, a big woman, came down the rough grassy slope from the house, a quick introduction took place, and Mrs. MacDonald and her car vanished.

For a moment I felt very much a displaced person.

But I need not have worried. Mrs. Madrowski was very easy to get on with, and was charming to me. She was young and bursting with health, and immensely fat. She wore thin brown slacks, stretched almost to breaking point, and a green shirt which was none too loose either.

She immediately took me on a tour of inspection, and I learned a great deal about herself, the farm, and the job. We wandered through the garden (I gathered there would be plenty of gardening for me), and into the yard. There seemed to be an endless supply of large black Labradors and half-grown puppies about: Mrs. Madrowski told me that her husband was trying to establish the breed in the district, but that he had not yet had much success: few people could a pure-bred Labrador, around here. The Madrowskis' pedigree Jersey herd, about twenty strong, was just now coming in for the evening milking, and together we tied them up in the spacious wooden barn. I was introduced to several friendly stable cats, one or two dogs, and finally to the Count himself, Col. Madrowski.

The Colonel was at least twenty years older than his wife, and even fatter. I had never seen such a colossal pair of people. I was afraid that if I worked here perhaps I should get that shape, too! I had a bad first impression of my would-be employer, for his face was quite terrifying and his manner abrupt; but his dogs obviously adored him, and he treated his cows as individuals, so I could forgive him a lot. He was very busy with the milking-machine, and had little time to talk; Mrs. Madrowski and I continued on our rounds. She took me into the dairy and showed me everything, but my mind was so full of new impressions that I found it impossible to concentrate on her detailed explanations of the evening and morning routines of weighing and cooling, recording, and sterilizing. One fact, however, I did absorb. That was that a great deal of my work would take place in the dairy among buckets and hot water – a point against the job.

Mrs. Madrowski told me how she and her husband had designed and built their own house and buildings, grown crops, and developed their herd; and I began to realize just how hard these backwoods farmers did have to work. Mrs. Madrowski shared most of the work with her husband: milking, feeding and mucking out; ploughing, sowing, and harvesting; buying, selling, and planning. In addition, she had her own special jobs of running the house, cooking, looking after the garden, working in the dairy – to mention only a few. Yet in comparison with other Canadian farmers' wives, she was not overworked, for she had the rare luxury of a governess for her two little girls.

I was to take over many of the routine jobs, such as dairy chores, and planting, weeding, and irrigating in the garden, in order that the Madrowskis might have more time for further developments and improvements in the farm. After a week or so, when I had "settled in" to the work, they would be able to go away together all day, whenever they wanted to buy new cattle and equipment, or to visit distant farms: I should be left in charge of the farm.

This business of being left in charge sounded attractive. I should merely go on with my gardening, keeping an eye open for the cows, and chasing them back to the pasture should they happen to break into the alfalfa or the garden. "And don't work too hard all the time," said Mrs. Madrowski. "Go for a ride on one of the ponies if you feel like it. They want riding, terribly badly. I never get time , these days."

I expressed huge surprise and delight, and was far from being put off by her subsequent casual mention of coyotes, wolves and bears. This was without a doubt the Wild West I had dreamt of; it was almost too good to be true!

When Mrs. Madrowski took me up the hill some way from the house, to show me the clean and sunny little wooden cabin that would be my bedroom, she made a remark that seemed to sum up the whole character of the place perfectly. "You needn't bother," she said, "to make a trip to the house in the mornings. Just go up into the bush, there's only the bears to see you."

The Madrowskis insisted on my staying to supper so that they could drive me down to Tappen afterwards. We ate in the kitchen. I watched Mrs. Madrowski cooking, and I watched them both eating, with fascination. They each had a great square of fried bread, two fried eggs, several thick slices of home-cured bacon, and a pool of hot fat from the frying-pan. I had considerable difficulty in persuading Mrs. Madrowski to give me only one piece of bacon and no "juice"; my plea for only one egg was laughed to scorn. "One egg! That's ridiculous!" she cried. "Anyway," added her husband gruffly, "you will have to learn to eat two if you are to be strong enough for farm work." I ate my two eggs.

Evidently there were few Canadian things Mrs. Madrowski did like: she was aggressively English in her tastes and habits. She kept to herself, spoke with a refined English accent and complete lack of Canadian expressions, and liked to feel that the neighbours thought her eccentric for having the only modern bathroom in the district.

Her husband was different: I do not believe he cared in the least what anybody thought. He was quite friendly towards me, but I felt instinctively that the friendliness was an effort to him, and would be dropped when I became his employee. I had a nasty feeling that he regarded me as an untouchable servant, and I had not the least doubt that he could be a merciless slave-driver.

I was glad when the time came for me to catch my 'bus; for it was long after dark, I was desperately tired, and I wanted above all to think things over in peace. We all three went down to Tappen in the Madrowski's car – Col. Madrowski driving, myself next to him "to discuss terms", and Mrs. Madrowski in the back. We left the farm dramatically, the car fairly leaping down the bumpy track, and the Count leaning out of his wide-open door, swearing ferociously in Polish at his dogs which were trying to follow. A few minutes later, as we came round a corner, two pairs of eyes suddenly gleamed red in the glare of our headlights, and as suddenly vanished.

" Wolves!" exclaimed Col. and Mrs. Madrowski in chorus.

I was too excited to speak. I pressed my face against the window, and caught sight of two grey forms slipping into the undergrowth. My first real wolves!

I almost made up my mind, then and there, to take the job. The pay sounded pretty poor; but after all, what would that matter, when I would be getting cow-bells and mountains, riding, wolves in the forest, and, in the mornings, only the bears to see me? But I had already told Mrs. Madrowski that I wanted to see my other possible job, and compare notes, and she had agreed that I should do this; so I made no promises. I just bid them farewell, and did the ten-mile 'bus journey in a sort of daze, my mind too full of new impressions to be capable of any kind of judgment.

It was after ten when I got back to my hotel in Salmon Arm. The old man said there had been no telephone call for me, but I wondered. I believed nobody had bothered to answer the telephone when it had rung. Surely Den would have kept his promise?

It was no use being angry; I decided to ring Den myself in the morning, and went to bed, where I sank at once into an exhausted and dreamless sleep.

CHAPTER EIGHT

On Saturday morning I tried to ring Den but there was no reply. I was disappointed, because he was going on down to Vancouver that evening, and I was afraid I had missed the chance of visiting his home with him and seeing his parents properly. In that brief meeting on Thursday night I had hardly begun to know them. I had been tired, they had been taken by surprise, and it had been too dark to see much: I was not even sure if I would recognize them again, now. How could I possibly expect them to be my friends, let alone as helpful as Den had told me they would be?

I went up to the Reporter office again but there were no further replies to my advertisement. Mr. Howard was interested to hear all about my visit to the Madrowskis, but he still seemed very keen that I should try the Harolds.

There was still no mail for me at the Post Office, and I felt rather flat. I tried to absorb myself in shopping, and found a drugstore with a good stationery department; I inspected the cheap books for a long time, but saw only one or two worth reading. Just as I was trying to make up my mind whether or not to spend a precious 35 cents on one of these, a familiar voice spoke just behind me:

"Hallo, Dina!"

I turned and found three brass blazer-buttons confronting me: Den was towering over me, bigger than ever. My, it was good to see him again! He said he was only in town for a few minutes now, but he would come down again to fetch me at 2:30, and I must come and see "his" mountain, and have tea with the family. We had a short mutual indignation meeting about the hotel proprietor, for Den had rung me while I was at the Madrowskis, and had left a message, which the old man had evidently forgotten. He had to hurry on to another store then, and I went off in high spirits.

Just round the corner I met his mother. I did recognize her at once, after all. Now I could see her in daylight at last, I noticed that she had Den's gentle and penetrating brown eyes. Although she must have been at least fifty, she looked young in a gay, yellow dress, and her dark, curly hair had only a suggestion of grey in it. We talked for a moment, and she was most friendly. I thought what a sweet face she had, and felt sure I was going to like her.

If only she would like me, too! She got into her car and drove off, and I went back to the hotel.

I was ready by 2:15, dressed, according to Den's instructions, in a tee-shirt and bluejeans. Now I was at last going to go up a mountain; now I was going right into The Bush! Maybe I would see deer tracks, maybe chipmunks – maybe even a bear. I was in a fever of suppressed excitement, and still a bit nervous about Den's parents. I sat in the entrance hall, pretending to read a newspaper, looking up anxiously whenever anyone walked past outside the open doors. Soon I began really reading, and when Den did arrive, punctually at 2:30, he was up the steps and inside the door before I saw him at all.

" That's right," he said, surveying my clothes approvingly. " Just the thing for the mountain."

" A bit odd for going out to tea with people for the first time, though?"

" Oh, shucks. They won't mind a bit. You don't need to worry about that."

As we drove out of town he asked how I was getting on, and I told him about the visit to the Madrowskis. He had not heard of them, but when I mentioned the Harolds his eyebrows went up. "Those people who live over on the other side of the lake? Well, what do you know! Do they have a farm?"

I said I imagined so, anyway I intended to find out for myself.

" I guess you'd find it too isolated over there."

" So do I. I expect I shall go to this place I saw yesterday; but I'm not going to miss the chance of seeing the Harold family." " I wish I could come with you. How many of them are there?"

In between questions, Den began pointing out landmarks. He showed me Mount Ida above the city, the Mount Ida of the photograph in the folder which had attracted me so much. He pointed out Bastion Mountain, still snow-capped, across the lake; then the turning which led to Canoe; and the position of his own home at the foot of the mountain ahead of us.

It was a five-mile drive, and nearly all uphill. The view grew lovelier and lovelier. Down on our left the lake shone white and blue, dreaming among its wooded mountains; and around us were houses and farms, orchards and little fields, and sometimes a patch of uncleared bush.

Suddenly, the main road swung off to the right at a crossroads, but we went bumping straight ahead, up a stony and rutted dirt road. There were no houses here, only green fields and more and more patches of wild woods and thickets; and the hedges were riotous with early summer growth.

At last we turned sharply, and the car laboured up a stony red drive between apple orchards in full bloom. Then there was a lawn with big spruce trees; a little, greyish-white, wooden house, half smothered in creepers and lilacs, nestling comfortably under the trees; and, rising immediately behind the house, the steep mountain-side and the bush.

Mrs. Meek came out to meet us and we went in at the kitchen door. Den rushed off to change, and I chatted to Mrs. Meek about yesterday's developments – the answers to my advertisement, the visit to Tappen. Everything was so informal that I was put completely at ease, even in those clothes. Den re-appeared in bluejeans and running shoes and we started off at once, Mrs. Meek seeing us off with motherly admonishments to be back in time for tea.

I did like Den's mountain. It was wild and jungly, and so steep, it seemed to me to be almost perpendicular. It was smaller than most of the other mountains nearby, and they were only small themselves, as mountains go; but it seemed huge to me. We went straight up it at Den's pace (nearly running), and got less than one-third of the way up in about 45 minutes. Sometimes we went through spruce and pine woods, sometimes through low, scrubby undergrowth open to the sun. Now and again Den would stop for a few moments, and I was glad, for I was getting a bit puffed, but would not for the world have admitted it. Later on, he told me he had stopped specially for me whenever he noticed I was not answering his remarks; but that he had been careful not to let me know his reasons in case I should be insulted.

Once he saw a chipmunk very close to, and tried hard to show it to me; but, try as I would, I could not see it. I was furious with myself.

We aimed at reaching the top of a rocky bluff half way up the mountain, which Den had pointed out to me from the car on the way up from Salmon Arm. We still had half an hour's climb ahead of us, when we came to a big isolated rock sticking up in the middle of a steep clearing. Den called it Wolf Rock. It was a superb view-point, and we scrambled to the top and sat together, looking out westwards over the great wooded mountains. Snow-streaked Bastion Mountain just showed through some young spruce trees on our right, dropping its huge red-dish cliffs sheer down into the lake. On Thursday night we had seen it from the train, looming darkly across the water, and Den had called it "a fine great chunk." The double peak of Mount Ida was on our left, and the long, rolling line of Spruce Hills ahead; while below us the civilized landscape was laid out like a map. There were green fields down there, white orchards, dark, spiky rows of trees, and deep green woods. Farmhouses were scattered about, and between them was a network of narrow white roads. Far away under Spruce Hills the little city of Salmon Arm was just visible beyond a low ridge.

From Den's mountain

Looking southwest, at Mt. Ida

Den showed me the road that wound its way to the southwest between our mountain and Mount Ida, and explained that twenty miles away it joined the Okanagan Valley. "That's a grand place," he said. "It goes right down to the U.S. border, and orchards all the way. Some call it Apple Valley; when you get B.C. Apples in England, that's where they mostly come from. It is in the arid zone, quite different from here, but it is all under irrigation. Mother loves it, she likes the open country. I prefer the woods, myself."

"So do I, much. But I should like to see the Okanagan, all the same."

"I think Mother and Dad might take you down in the car one day," he said. "They often go down to Kelowna, that is half-way down the valley, ninety miles from here. I'm sure you would love it."

Presently it was time to go on; but poor Den sprained his ankle jumping off the rock, and was terribly disappointed that we could not go on up to the bluff. Wolf Rock was good enough for me, but I knew how much Den had longed to show me his mountain right to the chosen place, and was sorry for him on that account as well as because of his ankle.

He bit his lip with the pain, and it flashed into my mind for the first time that he was very handsome. I wondered how on earth I had managed not to notice this before. I had been regarding his physical appearance merely as a vehicle for his personality, a label by which to recognize him.

"Here, I'll teach you a Wild West dodge," he said. He produced a penknife and I helped him to cut spruce branches and tie them in a bundle on which he could slide down the mountainside. The spruce, cut and bruised, smelt heavenly. But presently poor Den grew tired of tobogganing with his hurt leg held up. He almost succumbed to my offers of support, then said he was too heavy for me: he was a big man, indeed. Finally, he found a strong stick and came hobbling down with that.

We ended up in the next-door neighbour's orchard, where we stayed awhile and stared up into the blossom-laden branches while Den showed me chickadees and humming-birds. I loved the little brownish bird, first cousin to a bluetit, who said: "Chickadee, dee, chickadee, dee, dee-ee!" over and over again. And I had had no idea B.C. kept humming-birds. We watched a bright red one, no bigger than the top joint of a man's thumb, showing off before its hidden mate among the blossoms. It rose and fell, backed and advanced, and hung quivering in mid-air; its wings were visible only as a vague circle, a shadowy halo round the brilliant spark of its body. Now and again it called sharply, and the thin piping notes made a strange harmony with the low booming of its flight.

Den rested his hand on my shoulder and we watched in silence and peace, moving no muscle lest we disturb the humming-bird, breathing not a word because words were unnecessary. We both saw, we both loved and understood what we saw, why should we speak? Never before had I found such a congenial sharer of silences, never such a peaceful and wholly adequate companionship. But when the hen-bird rose whirring from the blossoms and the male followed her to another tree, I stepped down the hill away from Den. I was suddenly afraid of too much happiness too soon: there must be no regrets on this adventure of mine. Den did not touch me again and I was grateful for his understanding.

We went back to the house and ate a huge tea with his parents in their kitchen, which served also as dining-room. Mr. Meek sat opposite me. He was tall and quiet, and had blue eyes and straight, grey hair; he appeared to be ten or fifteen years older than his wife. Den had inherited his father's build but his mother's hair and eyes.

Self, Den Meek, Mr. Meek, Mrs. Meek (Margery

After tea we moved into the sitting-room. Mr. Meek and I discovered that we both knew a particular obscure Devonshire village, and were soon deep in reminiscences. Now the last of the ice was broken: there was no doubt that we were all going to like each other very much. Mr, and Mrs. Meek shared Den's view about the Harolds. "You wouldn't like it," they said. "Why, you'd be buried alive!"

Den and his mother came down to town with me in the car and left me at the hotel at about seven o'clock. Mrs. Meek had already promised to take me to Kelowna if she and her husband went next week. They expected to go on Monday, and if I would give them a ring next day, Sunday, they would let me know.

Den was to leave that evening on the night train; but he intended to come home for a long weekend in September. We parted without even shaking hands, and made a date to climb to the very top of "his" mountain in September. "In the meantime," he said, "may I write to you now and again?"

Two days later I wrote to a friend in England:

"Den has given me a wonderful introduction to Salmon Arm, and two good friends in his parents; he has already introduced me to many B.C. animals and flowers, and has recommended suitable field-books so I can study these. Also, he will be home for a weekend in the autumn, when he has promised to take me up to the top of his mountain. So I shall stay out West till the autumn quite definitely...."

CHAPTER NINE

Sunday morning. I was suddenly wide awake at six o'clock, and before I even opened my eyes I knew it was one of those beautiful sunny mornings on which it is a crime to stay in bed. I dressed, let myself out of the front door quietly,and went down towards the station. The sun was already well up over the mountains, but none in the little city was awake, save myself and the chirping sparrows. The broad street seemed broader than usual, and so quiet that I was glad I had crepe rubber soles and need not go tap-tapping along the sidewalk. I went to the end of the railway platform, crossed the tracks, and followed a stony road which took me under the row of poplar trees and onto the beginning of a long wooden wharf. There were big marshy fields on either side, one of them full of nice little Aberdeen Angus cows, sleek and black and shiny. I wandered on for what seemed a long time.

Although the fields looked flat they dropped away gradually, so that the wharf on its wooden struts rose higher and higher above them. Soon I was looking down on mud-flats with rushes and wading birds, and I wondered if the lake ever rose far enough to reach the edge of the field where the cattle were grazing. I supposed it must, otherwise why should the wharf begin so far back?

I walked on, and at last there was water underneath, instead of mud, and the wharf widened out abruptly. A little old wooden hut, grey and weather-beaten, crouched on the wide place, and beyond it a slipway ran down into the water. Small boats were moored nearby, and a big wooden boathouse stood right in the water.

The view was exquisite. Shuswap Lake broadens at the western end to a width of ten miles; I stood alone on the end of the wharf in the warm early morning sunshine and gazed out across those ten miles of brilliant water until my eyes were dazzled. From so near the surface the little bumpy hills ranged across the north shore looked only one mile away, not ten; but they were so purply-blue and misty that I knew their smallness must be an illusion of distance. They did look so unimportant beside the great wooded mountains at this end.

Bastion Mountain, red and rocky, glowered fiercely over the water. Just under it, I knew, the lake narrowed and stretched back eastwards past Canoe to Sicamous and beyond that, northwards to Mosquito Creek; but from here the opening was hidden by a low point of land nearby. The railway curved round the edge of the bay and disappeared over this headland: I could see the gap in the trees where it went through, the very gap I had come through three days before, and from which I had first caught sight of the lights of Salmon Arm. I went down the slipway and put my hands in the water. My lake!

Then I turned and looked back to the south. The wharf ran back, tapering with perspective, to end in the distant row of poplars which hid the city. The low-lying fields made a big, dry bay which must at one time have been part of the lake bed. Beyond them were gentle slopes with fields and houses, woods and orchards; then the timbered mountains rose up: Den's mountain on the left, Spruce hills on the right and Mount Ida in the middle, thrusting bare, red rocks out above its trees.

Hundreds of little brown martins were swooping around me, and building the beginnings of their mud nests under the eaves of the boathouse and the old hut. I watched them until I grew hungry, then walked back to the hotel.

After breakfast I went out again, and this time I strolled for an hour or so through the little roads at the back of the town, admiring everybody's lovely unfenced gardens. It was my favourite season, everywhere there were lilacs and greenness, and in a waste place I found more wild tulips in the grass.

While I walked I began to have an idea.

At ten o'clock I rang the Meeks form the hotel: they still did not know whether they would be going to Kelowna tomorrow, and asked me to ring again in the evening.

My idea developed into a plan. It was a wild plan, but I would carry it out, all the same. I would try to get over to the Harold's farm today, not wait till Thursday. I would go to Canoe first, although there were no buses: after all, what were six and a half miles when I had all day? There was nothing else to do but go for a long walk, and I might as well walk to Canoe as anywhere. And when I got there, I might find somebody fishing, or just messing around in a boat, who would not mind giving me a lift across the lake. Somehow I felt sure there would be somebody. The lake was only a mile across in that part; and, once on the far shore, I could walk along and find the farm on my own.

I set off up the main road the way Den had driven me the day before. Up and up and up I trudged, hot but happy in the blazing sun. There was hardly any traffic today to stir the dust on the road. After about an hour I took what I thought was the Canoe turning. It was a narrow lane, white and stony and dusty, and dead straight. As I followed it it seemed to grow longer and longer, while I grew hotter and hotter and apparently made no progress at all. I began to wonder if it would ever come to an end. There were masses of wild roses in the hedges, deeper pink than our English ones, and I saw some humming-birds again. Once I stopped to talk to a friendly Jersey cow over a fence.

At last the road literally came to an end, in a wood. Realizing that the Canoe road must be further over to my right, I cut across country to join it, and was glad of the break. In an open place I saw two ground-hogs chasing each other in and out of a big pile of brushwood; and in a pine wood I found a Lady's Slipper, surely the loveliest of all Canadian wild flowers. The cool shade of the pines was welcome after those miles of dusty road, and I was not hurrying. Suddenly I came upon it, alone among the damp pine-needles on the dark soil, just one Lady's Slipper. It was the only one I ever saw, and there was no mistaking it. A perfect little slipper, it was – one could imagine it had been taken straight from a fairy's foot and hung by the top of the heel to a delicate stalk. Only one slipper, deep purple, with pointed toe and long, curled-back tongue, poised six inches above the cool black earth. I sat down to admire it for several minutes, and though I left it untouched it is still with me, and so is the elfin joy of finding it.

It was after twelve when I got to Canoe, and I went straight across the railway towards the wharf. Mrs. Howard had told me of a Mr. and Mrs. Pitt who owned a boating and fishing camp, and I searched them out at once and explained my plans. Mrs. Pitt was plump and cheerful and had a English Midlands accent. She knew the Harolds, especially the daughter, Jessie, and insisted on bringing me into her front room for a cup of tea and a piece of cake, while she chatted about the Harolds, and about the "Old Country."

I was lucky about my lift. A couple by the name of Anderson were just about to go out on a fishing trip in one of Mr. Pitt's motor boats, and they would take me, of course! They took me, not only across to the other shore, but the full three miles up lake to the Harolds' place, and assured me that they would fetch me back on their way home in the late afternoon.

I was enchanted with the Harold family. They were not in the least put out when I blew in, unannounced, just in time for Sunday lunch. They paid no attention to my murmurings about having had cake with Mrs. Pitt, but made me come in and share their meal. The living room was rough and ready, but the cloth on the square table was of exquisite damask linen, and the family table-manners were perfect.

The old Doctor was white-haired, and had piercing, greeny-blue eyes and a cashmere sweater to match them. Mrs. Harold was stout and kindly but pathetically stooped over, half crippled with years of work. She and her husband must both have been about eighty. Buster and Jessie, the son and daughter, told me they were forty-five and forty-three years old, and insisted that I call them by their Christian names right from the start.

Jessie wore glasses, and her greying hair was drawn back severely into a bun; but her figure was strong and boyish with hard work, and I soon found her to be anything but severe. Buster was strong and weather-beaten, but there was infinite kindness in his eyes, and he handled his animals with a gentleness I had seldom seen in any man.

Both he and Jessie were soft-spoken, and pussy-quiet in all their movements – true children of the Canadian forest. They lived out here since they were babies, and the farm and the lake and the bush were the whole of life to them. After lunch they showed me quickly round the farm and buildings, and I could see how much the farm meant to them, and how badly they needed help. Buster wanted extra time off from work this year, to start on the staggering project of building a new house for this parents to enjoy in their last years – building it himself!

The farm consisted of thirty acres of cleared, level land on the lake shore, at the foot of a wild forested mountain. There was a little herd of Jersey cows, two work horses, hens, pigs, fruit- trees, a big vegetable garden, pasture and hay. The cows grazed out on the mountainside in the summer, and the farm was practically self-supporting. Everything was home made, even the threshing machine, a complicated affair which Buster showed me with true craftsman's pride.

I should be required to work the horses, and do gardening and milking. It would certainly be interesting to work for these people, I thought, if I could stand the lack of baths and electricity and other amenities; but I wondered if I could bear the isolation. The place was cut off by the lake in front and the steep virgin forests behind, and the nearest neighbours lived over a mile away. I should be entirely dependent on the Harolds and their small boat for transport to Canoe, a good half-hour's trip across the lake; while over the remaining six and a half miles from there to Salmon Arm there were only four buses a day, and none at all on Wednesdays and Sundays.

Letters could only be mailed or collected once a week, when Buster and Jessie did the family shopping in Salmon Arm. Would I like this kind of life? I had many doubts.

Buster and Jessie kept talking about "the canyon," and were obviously bursting to show it to me. Eventually they decided we would have time if we were quick, and the Andersons could wait if they came for me too soon: they and I could all stop to tea.

We set out along the top of the fields, Buster and Jessie stopping every now and then to pick up a stick off their future hay crop, and fling it into the bush. I wondered whatever the "canyon" was going to be like. At the end of the last field, about a quarter of a mile from the house, we dived into the bush, and were in the canyon immediately. It was all on the Harolds' property, and down it came the "creek" which was their water supply, now a fierce gushing river. "We'll take your right to the top," said Buster and Jessie. "You must see the falls."

The Falls in Herald's Canyon
(Margaret falls)   on Reinecker Creek

It was a canyon, indeed. It was beautiful but also terrifying. I had never been anywhere so utterly wild. The rock cliffs towered over us on either side and the spruces between them were the most enormous trees I had ever seen. It was all cool and shady, and full of old fallen trunks and festoons of hanging moss, strange undergrowth, and perilous places to be climbed. We had to keep crossing the creek, walking along wet, slippery, fallen trunks high above the water with nothing to hold. A fall might have been fatal.

The Falls in Herald's Canyon
(Margaret falls) on Reinecker Creek

Jessie and Buster, who had been up and down here all their lives, thought nothing of it; but I was nearly sick with fear and with not letting them think I cared, and felt I deserved the V.C. afterwards. At the top, Buster took off his shoes and carried me across the creek to get a better view of the falls, which came into the canyon at right angles to it; it took two or three minutes each way, as he had to feel so carefully for safe footing at every step. I was scared, but it was worth it to see those falls.

High, high above us – above the tops of the great cliffs on either side – the water foamed out from a narrow gorge and came hurtling down over the rocks, a shaking white streak, to fall into a great round hollow it had made for itself in the cliff. From the high pool in the hollow, it spilled over again, and spread out transparently as it streamed down the last thirty feet of rock onto the canyon floor. Everything around us was wet with the perpetual rain of spray, and the thunderous roaring echoed and re-echoed between the cliffs, making conversation impossible.

We returned the same way, and I was terrified again, and could not help being glad when we came out into the warm meadows away from those towering cliffs. But I felt I had done something worth doing, something I should never forget. When Buster told me he thought I had done very well for a newcomer, I glowed with pride.

On the way back to the house I told them I would come and try the job for a week. It just seemed that I had no choice. The Harolds were special people, they needed me so badly, and they seemed so certain I would come. I hated to hurt their feelings! When two people like Buster and Jessie show one their private pride and joy, and when the private pride and joy is something so terribly beautiful, so beautifully terrible, as the Harolds' canyon, it is as if they have shown one their own souls; one cannot think of refusing them help as though they were just any old prospective employers. Of course I would come.

The Andersons were already waiting when we got back, and Mrs. Harold gave us all a big tea. When Buster and Jessie saw me off from their little one-plank wharf, it was arranged that I should come next Thursday; Jessie would herself meet me in Salmon Arm.

" Anyway," she said reassuringly, "if you find you don't like us, you can say so; and if we don't like you, we can say so. But I'm sure we shall all like each other."

I did not feel at all reassured. I knew just how difficult it would be to break away from such people without hurting their feelings and my conscience. Afterwards I had dreadful qualms, and wondered what on earth I had let myself in for. "But it's only for a week," I told myself, not very convincingly. "Of course I can leave if I can't stand it."

Suddenly I remembered about working the horses, and it occurred to me - rather late - that I had never in my life harnessed a farm horse. I hoped I should not make a fool of myself.

Then I thought of all the advantages: I should get to know the Harolds better, I should be living in just the kind of Wild West house I had dreamed of, I should be on the shore of my dream lake, and at the foot of my dream mountain. The bush would be all around me, as wild as anyone could wish; I should learn from Buster and Jessie the names of dozens of strange new animals, plants and butterflies; and Buster had promised to teach me to fish. There was also a materialistic but important consideration: I should be paid fifteen dollars a month more than the Madrowskis had offered. Above all, this job was a unique opportunity, an experience not to be missed. Maybe in a month's time I should leave, and earn still more on thinning and fruit picking jobs down the Okanagan.

I was tired by the time we reached Canoe, and extremely grateful when the Andersons offered to take me on to

Salmon Arm in their car; I wondered sleepily how I should ever have managed that walk a second time.

That evening I rang Mrs. Meek from the hotel. She said she was not going to Kelowna tomorrow, but might do so on Wednesday. She was amazed when I told her I had been over to the Harolds', and even more astonished when I said I was going to give the job a trial. "You'll find it dreadfully isolated," she said.

"I know," I replied. "But it's only for a week's trial. I don't expect I shall stay on."

But inside me, I wondered. I found myself hoping and praying Mrs. Meek would be able to take me to Kelowna on Wednesday, almost as if I felt Wednesday would be the last day of freedom in my whole life.

I went to bed, considerably sobered down.

CHAPTER TEN

On Monday I took it easy for a change. I went shopping in the morning, and bought a tough pair of shoes for work; then I called on Mr. Howard, who was obviously pleased I had chosen the Harolds rather than the Madrowskis. I tried to visit Mrs. Meek, who helped the family income by hairdressing on her own in town. I found the door, with her name stencilled on the frosted glass and BEAUTY SHOPPE underneath, but it was locked.

At the Post Office, joy of joys, my first mail was awaiting me. There were three letters from England and one from my sister in Toronto. I had in a way been dreading mail, because I knew it would shake me out of the blissful state I had been in since leaving Toronto a week before, and make me feel the first twinge of loneliness. It did, but it was unspeakably welcome, nevertheless. I read the letters over and over again, and spent all the afternoon answering them.

In the evening I went to the little cinema, delighting in my extravagance.

"I shall soon be earning dollars," I told myself, "and as long as I work over at the Harolds' I shall have nothing whatever to spend them on."

I whiled away the next morning, sitting down on the wharf and wandering about in the broad, dusty streets of the little Western town. I watched each train come roaring into the station and, immense and full of importance, stand steaming there, while the bell up on the front of its engine swung to and fro, clang, clang, clang, clang, never stopping until it was time to move off again.

In Salmon Arm the trains were specially exciting, for every time one came in the whole place quivered as if a frightful earthquake were beginning. During my first night there I thought the hotel must be on its last legs, for, although the railway was quite 200 yards away, the trains made the whole building rock, and my window vibrated horribly. Soon, however, I grew so used to this phenomenon that I ceased to notice it. Mrs. Meek told me that it was caused by the city being built on a thin crust over muskeg, or swamp, from which the lake had long ago receded: a town built on a great quaking bog!

In the afternoon I went to Mrs. Meek's "office" (she hated the name "Beauty Shoppe", which the decorators had painted on the door in her absence); I went as a customer, but Mrs. Meek insisted on shampooing my hair as a gift - "a B.C. Gift," she called it.

"Do you still want to come to Kelowna with us?" she asked. "We're going tomorrow, but we have to start early."

"I'll be ready any time you say," I said.

The Meeks collected me in their car shortly after seven next morning. Kelowna is ninety miles from Salmon Arm, and the drive took us nearly four hours. Distances mean nothing in Canada, for the land is so thinly populated: in all those ninety miles we passed through no more than four towns, only one of which was bigger than Salmon Arm.

It was a wonderful drive. We climbed for the first thirty miles, and after that the road lay downhill, or level, almost all the way. The woods began to thin out, and as we came near the small town of Enderby a tremendous view opened up in front of us, of a broad, level valley, with a lazy river curving this way and that between wide fields, and a timbered mountain ridge sheltering the fields on either side. On one ridge there was a mass of reddish cliffs. "Those are Enderby Crags," said Mrs. Meek. "You must notice them on the way back, because they can be quite incredible when the sunset light catches them; I've seen them when everything was dark around me, standing out like a great fire up there."

The Meeks pointed out the clear river at Enderby, peaceful beneath its willow trees, "so like England." Once we had a glimpse of far distant white mountains, up a long valley behind us. All the time the lines of the landscape grew smoother, broader, more gentle, as the countryside opened out and the timbered mountains gave way to low, barren hills. By the time we reached Vernon we were among the brown hills Mrs. Meek loved so much; and between the hills orchards and green fields spread themselves luxuriously over broad sweeps of open land. "There is such a wonderful feeling of space down here," said Mrs. Meek. "I miss that so much among all those forests at Salmon Arm." The further we went, the happier she grew. She told me how beautiful the hills were later in the summer, all golden-brown like sea sand in the sun, with the deep blue sky behind them. But I believed I liked them better now, dressed as they were in the faintest, green gauze film of grass.

Soon we came to the lakes. Kalamalka, eight or nine miles long, was the loveliest. Never have I seen such exquisite colours in water: deep blues, jade, turquoise and emerald green, and, rippling among them, a thousand shattered fragments of reflection from the hillside beyond, green-brown with a freckling of dark pines. Mrs. Meek said that sometimes the water was like glass, unruffled, and the mirrored image of the hillside lay as still as the hillside itself. Perhaps it would be like that when we came home that evening. The most wonderful sight she had ever seen was Kalamalka under a red sunset sky. The colours in the water were always changing: in all the many times she had been past here she had never seen them the same twice. The name, Kalamalka, means "Lake of Many Colours."

At Kelowna we were still among Mrs. Meek's beloved brown hills, bare but for the occasional speckling of pines. Between them lay a sheet of sparkling water, part of seventy-mile long Okanagan Lake. We had lunch together in a hotel, then while the Meeks did their business I explored Kelowna. It is the fourth largest city in British Columbia. I admired it for its clean looks, its broad main street, and all its weeping willows, but I preferred to be away from houses and traffic. I wandered around the public park, and eventually took the ferry-boat across the lake and went for a walk along the far shore, where I went into private ecstasies over my first Swallowtail and Camberwell Beauty butterflies

We drove back in the evening, stopping for supper on the way, and arriving in Salmon Arm after sunset. Kalamalka's colours had changed with the changing light and were even more beautiful than before, and the reflections were unbroken. When we went through Enderby the Crags were ablaze with red and purple: Mrs. Meek said they were not at their best, but they seemed brilliant enough to me.

It was long after dark when I came into the hotel. The Meeks had driven on down to the town, four miles past their own turning, to bring me right to my doorstep. What kind people, and what a happy day!

Thursday, June 1st was an anti-climax day": it was bound to be, after such a drive. When I should have been feeling nothing but gratefulness I felt miserable. I sat in the gloomy hotel lobby, my two packed suitcases beside me, and tried half-heartedly to write letters. I had had a very full week, and just now I was in a horrid, lonely gap between those carefree days and a job about which I was full of misgivings. I always get excited about new experiences, it is true, but when I actually have to face them the excitement dies: more often than not I hate the process of setting out on a new phase of life.

It was now two-thirty, and at about four o'clock I was literally going to launch forth into the unknown. Buster and Jessie Harold were probably in town already; soon I should have to make some effort to contact them.

I made calculations on the blotting paper. I had been seven nights in that hotel, which had cost me $17.50, excluding meals. It was high time I did some earning! In any case, I felt it was time I did rather less taking and more giving.

Just as I opened my case to put away my writing-pad in walked Jessie Harold herself.

CHAPTER ELEVEN

Jessie had come into town without Buster. She and I sat in the sun on a grassy bank by the railway and ate bananas, and at four o'clock we went down onto the wharf. The boat was there and due to start, but no sign of the captain. In the next half-hour three or four more passengers arrived and began pacing up and down the wharf, but it was after five-thirty when the captain turned up, grinning happily and breathing beer; and it was almost six when we at last got going.

I had had no idea the trip would be so long : it took us the best part of two hours. The old ferry- boat chugged around headlands and into bays, calling in at I don't know how many little lakeside houses to drop the odd passenger or two. Just as I thought we must be nearly there, it went back across the lake to Canoe to pick up several more passengers. It was pushing a heavy scow in front, and the stopping and starting and turning all took a long time, to say nothing of the loading and unloading of various goods. It was a private boat, Jessie told me, which did a weekly ferry service covering all the lake shore houses from Sicamous to Salmon Arm. "The Captain calls at every house that puts a flag out for him," she said.

Jessie kept making conversation, and I tried to respond brightly, but without much success. I felt perfectly miserable. I left her in the warm cabin and escaped onto the deck alone, with the excuse that I wanted to look at the mountains. I stayed up there until I grew cold; but just then I almost hated even the mountains, and found myself actually fighting back stupid tears. I was afraid of the unknown, and lonely with the kind of loneliness that only deepens when strangers try to help.

It was almost eight when we at last arrived, and I had to start in to work almost at once, helping with a long and laborious dish-washing after supper. It seemed to me more like hard work, and less like "just helping" than any other dish-washing I had ever taken part in. However, Dr. And Mrs. Harold were kind to me; and when I found I was to sleep in my own private cabin, separate from the house, I was so pleased that I forgot all my troubles. Jessie, full of unnecessary apologies about my accommodation, helped me to carry blankets and sheets across the lawn from the house and make up my bed. Like the ferry trip and the dish washing, this was a lengthy business, and it was after eleven when I climbed, gratefully, into bed.

Next morning I was up at 6:15 to help Buster with the cows before breakfast, milking two of them myself. There were nine Jerseys, ranging from half-grown heifers to old cows, but only three were in milk at present. How good it was to be milking again!

I liked working for Buster, he was so quiet and gentle. After breakfast he harnessed Duke to the horse-hoe and we did a very thorough cultivation of the raspberry bed: up and down we went between the rows all the morning. Buster managing the hoe while I walked beside him driving the horse. It was grand to be holding a pair of reins once more. I was quite sure I was going to enjoy this job.

My cabin, with lilies of the valley

In my first spare half-hour I went to sit in my own little cabin. Lunch was over, but Mrs. Harold was not yet ready for me to help her wash up. It was the most charming log cabin you could imagine: of real, genuine, unadorned logs, and built in 1882! It was grey with weathering, and had a belonging look about it, almost as if it had grown there. Flowers and shrubs grew against it, and the roof slanted down to low eaves on either side; near the top a funny little iron chimney stuck up, like the chimney on a gypsy caravan. Inside, it was very dry and quite warm enough; and just the right size for a bedroom, snug but not cramped. It contained my bed, two low benches, a small table, a chair, and a stove in the middle. There was a wide bench all along one side, covered with all manner of tools and junk, with firewood and old newspapers stacked underneath it, and horseshoes hanging on nails above it. In one corner was a huge drill such as one sees in blacksmiths' shops: Buster called it the "post drill."

My cabin and the house---- and Dr. Herald's back

Along the middle of the cabin the roof was too high for me to reach, but if I moved more than a yard to either side I bumped my head on it, and when I went to make my bed I had to crouch right down. At one end there was a wide, heavy door with a small fixed window beside it; and at the other, an openable window. At night I lit myself to bed with an Aladdin oil-lamp.

From my seat at the table I could look out of the open door and down across a narrow strip of alfalfa meadow, to a row of tall trees with the lake gleaming behind them.

Unfortunately, the trees hid most of the view; but between and above them I could pick out the wooded mountains on the other side of the lake, and, just showing high over the forests in the distance, two snow peaks which must surely have been over twenty miles away, perhaps thirty or even forty.

Behind me, outside the other window, there was a flat meadow with a strip of ploughed land, and a few fruit-trees, backed with a row of white poplars and birches. Immediately behind the birches the mountain rose up nearly sheer, covered with great spruce and cedar trees from top to bottom – the home of ground-hogs and chipmunks, bears, flying squirrels, deer and even cougars: all kinds of exciting animals. I longed to see some of them. I was already delighting in the big

Swallowtail and Camber well Beauty butterflies that seemed as common here as Cabbage Whites; and I was getting to know some of the plants. Jessie had pointed out flowers and shrubs to me during the walk up the Canyon on Sunday, and I was adding new names to the list begun by Den. Many of these names were as lovely as the flowers themselves: twin flower, brown- eyed Susan, salmon berry, ocean spray.

Things were truly primitive here. The Harolds' wooden house (they themselves called it "the old shack") had one room downstairs with a curtained-off part which served as Dr. and Mrs. Harold's bedroom; over it was a loft divided with a curtain into two rooms for Jessie and Buster. In the loft there were no chests of drawers, no closets, but only open shelves; and downstairs there was an ancient sofa, a piano, a glass- fronted cupboard full of china, and a cluttered

writing-desk.

The water-supply came along a high, raised wooden trough (a "flume") which crossed the field on wooden posts, from the creek. Buster had laid pipes to the kitchen tap and the garden hose, but elsewhere all water had to be carried. The Harolds did own a washing machine (run by petrol engine) but it had to be fed with kettles.

Before I had been in the job twenty-four hours I realized that I had come into a very full, real life, a life which made more so-called civilized ways seem soft and artificial. Here I was managing, and would have to go on managing, without many things I had hitherto thought essential; and I was already doing many things I would not have believed possible.

That first afternoon found me standing on the top of a sledge full of branches I had loaded myself, driving both horses off over the grass to the bonfire site. "Are you sure you can trust the Toronto typist with all this lot?" I had asked Buster before I set off. "Toronto typists aren't often so good with horses," he replied. I glowed with pride, for I knew he meant it, because they did not go in for flattery or white lies, a word of praise from one of the Harolds was worth a lot.

I found I could drive a team of two quite easily, although I had never done it before. I knew now that I would never have to harness them myself. "I wouldn't dream of letting you do it," Buster had said. "The gear is all for too heavy for you to lift."

"It has been worth it," I wrote home late that night, "worth saying I was experienced with horses and then keeping quiet about the details. Other things have been worth doing, too: walking six and a half wild miles and asking brazenly, at a strange house at Sunday lunch-time, for a three- mile lift across the lake; controlling my nerves in that wonderful canyon; taking on this job at all - oh, everything I have done here has been worth it!"

The house, like a shabby old mother hen, held out a ragged wing of roof under which the kitchen crouched for shelter. Under the same scant protection was a broad alley-way which led right through from the garden to the back yard, separating the kitchen from the house.

The alley-way was cloakroom, larder, hall, tool-shed and kennel all rolled into one. At each end of it was a large door, far from weatherproof but usually open anyway; inside were a washing machine, a low bench covered with milk pails, and walls hung with everything from milk jugs and garden tools to Buster's old raincoat. Here the dogs would lie to avoid both the blazing June sun and the stifling heat of the kitchen, here the cats would queue up for meals, and here, too, the hens would wander in and out making vague and stupid hen- noises until someone bothered to chase them out. Two other rickety wooden doors opened from the alley-way: one into the house and one into the kitchen.

Whenever I think of the Harolds' farm I think first of that kitchen, for it was the hub round which all their life revolved. It was a large, square room with windows to the north and south, a door to the east, and an enormous range in an alcove in the west wall. I had it orientated in my mind like this, for the Harolds seemed to think of everything in terms of the points of the compass, and life with them was difficult until one learnt to do the same.

Although the kitchen was furnished with only the range, a table, a cupboard, and one or two shelves, the space was well filled. The walls, of bare, round logs dark with age and dust, were covered with milk pans, tin basins, and gigantic cooking-pots hanging on various nails. The floor, of rough well-worn wood, was usually dirty, but one could not see much of it on account of the veritable forest of dogs and pails all over it.

Often I counted fifteen, even nineteen, pails on the kitchen floor at one time: pig-pails, milk- pails, calf-buckets, buckets made from big lard-cans, slop buckets for the wash-basin. And the dogs! Full-sized sheep-dogs stretched out on a kitchen floor can take up more space than one would think.

Jessie with Lassie and family. "Judge" in center front

There was a praiseworthy piece of Buster's home plumbing by the north window: a pipe with two taps on it, and a shallow sink with a real drain. These were very special, for in the Harolds' house they were the only taps, the only pipe, and the only drain. The taps faced opposite ways, one over the sink and the other muzzled with a piece of white linen for a strainer, over the drinking-water tub.

The kitchen range, huge and black, dominated everybody and everything. It cooked the food, heated the great kettles which were the only source of hot water, aired the clothes, warmed people and dogs when they were cold, and dried them when they were wet. But for these services it got its own back on everybody. It kept its own private wood-pile in a corner beside it, and Buster had to spend hours, summer and winter, splitting and carrying wood to replenish this.

The stove burnt Mrs. Harold's fingers on every possible occasion; brought out beads of sweat on her forehead instead of contenting itself with heating the food; and blackened her cooking-pots dreadfully. Worst of all, its heat was an open invitation to every mosquito on the lake to spend the evenings in the kitchen.

Washing up, supervised jointly by the stove and Mrs. Harold, was a very solemn and important rite. It was not carried on, as one might have expected, at the sink. Dear me, no, the sink was far too great a luxury to be used for such messy jobs, and none but the cleanest water must be allowed to enter that precious and perhaps block able drain. No. Washing up took place on the table, and the dirty water had to go into buckets.

I can still see it all so clearly. It is about to begin. Mrs. Harold sits on a tall stool ("I used to stand to all my chores, Lavender, but now I sit when I can. It's my back. When Jes and I saw Dr. Holmes he said..."). In front of the old lady the table groans with dirty plates, cups, glasses, knives and forks, and huge "platters;" while amongst the dogs and pails on the floor there lurks an ominous crowd of huge and dirty cooking-pots, waiting..... Mrs. Harold reaches behind her and places on the table a blackened horror which turns out to be an ancient and well- flattened wash-powder (Dreft) box.

"Now, Lavender, I'm ready for the dishpan, please."

Dishpan, dishpan. I look wildly round at the walls, which are fairly covered with large pans. If I know anything about the Harolds, only one of those pans could conceivably be the dishpan. Ah! That nice, deep, white one now, on the nail near the woodpile –

"No, Lavender, on the stove."

On the stove! Of course, but how stupid. Stepping gingerly between the dogs, I fetch from the hotplate the big shallow pan of steaming soapy water and place it on Mrs. Harold's Dreft-box mat. .

"Thank you. Now that pan on the North wall, please. No, Lavender, the North wall. That's right – no, by woodpile. Yes, the top one. Over here on my right, please; thank you."

The empty pan is duly placed beside the other, and you would think we could proceed. But no. "Now, Lavender, would you get me a little cold water, please." Always polite, dear Mrs. Harold. I thread my way once more between the dogs and pails, fetching a dipper full of drinking-water from the tub, adding the exact amount required by Mrs. Harold to cool her washing-up water, and returning the dipper to its own particular nail.

Aha! Mrs. Harold has filled her dishpan with glasses and forks, and is already placing the washed up things in the empty pan to drain. Wonderful! We have got going at last. I seize a cloth and bear down joyfully on the first glass.

"Wait a minute, Lavender, they must be scalded first. You kin jest sit down a minute and rest yourself while I get this pan full."

Meekly I obey, and watch the draining-pan filling up. Draining-pan, did I say? Although the plates are jammed in edgewise, every glass or cup is right side up and could not possibly be draining. Things are packed into that pan as nobody but a Harold could pack them; and when there is no room for anything bigger than an acorn-cup my enforced rest comes to an end at last.

"Now you kin scald them, Lavender. But jest fetch me that other pan from by the woodpile first, please, and I kin be filling it while you do these."

She pushes the full pan across the table and I replace it with the other; then I go to the range for the big kettle. Whew, it is heavy! I have to take tremendous care not to stumble over the dogs with it, as I might scald them, not to mention myself. I pour boiling water over and into the washed things, even the glasses, until at last Mrs. Harold is satisfied; then I return the kettle to the range.

Now, surely, you would think I could begin drying up. But, believe it or not, another soul-destroying routine must first be performed: Filling the Kettle. This is the last word in patience-tests, and must always proceed as follows: --

1. Take the lid off the big pot at the back of the stove, and balance it somewhere cleanish.

2. Take the lid off the kettle and hang on to it (for lack of anywhere else cleanish).

3. Fetch the dipper from the other side of the room.

4. Fill the kettle from the big pot (at least four dipper fulls).

5. Step back and forth among the dogs, fetching one dipper full after another of cold water to refill the big pot.

My, what a relief to do some good old, ordinary drying up! Soon the pan is empty, the clean, dry things balanced in every bit of available space, and the drained-off water poured away down the sink. Then follows the second pan full, entailing a complete repetition of scalding, Filling the Kettle, and drying up. After that come the knives, which for some mysterious reason are placed, all soapy, straight on the table, and may be dried without scalding.

By this time Mrs. Harold has progressed as far as the cooking-pots from the floor, and I embark on a trial-and-error system of putting things away, directed by Mrs. Harold from her stool. But that is a subject in itself.

CHAPTER TWELVE

They were remarkable people, the Harolds. They were true pioneers, and had gone through more than their fair share of hardship; it had left them full of strength of character, wisdom, amazing practical capability and enough stories to fill a library.

Dr. Harold was wonderful at eighty. He had done his medical training at Queen's University at Kingston, Ontario, and was a fully qualified doctor. He had practised in Vancouver long years back, when the great city of today was still undreamed of, and when Fourth Avenue was but a trail through the bear-haunted bush. He had done his rounds on horseback, and was still full of tales about those long, muddy, adventurous rides.

But he gave up his profession. On holiday once, he fell in love with Shuswap Lake, and nothing would do but he must live on its shores. Unlike most of us, he put his dreams into practice: he acquired a large piece of mountainside under virgin forest, cleared a little patch of land, built his wooden house, and brought his wife and baby to live there. And there they had lived for forty- four years. Jessie came as a baby, Buster and another son were born on the place; and from the first time they could move around at all, those children had had to help with the chores. The boys had helped in the heartbreaking, backbreaking job of clearing land. Little by little they had pushed back the frontiers of the forest until they had those thirty acres; and gradually, very gradually, they were still expanding: there were two new clearings in the woods to the east of the house.

Lassie + Prince in the basement

The children had grown up without ever seeing the inside of a church or a school; but from their parents, between chores, they had learned to read and write and do sums, to fear God and keep holy the Sabbath day, and to mind their manners. Arthur had married young and gone to live in the States, but Buster and Jessie had stayed on. This was their life, and any other life would have terrified them. They remembered their visit to Vancouver, Jessie's second and Buster's first one, a year or two before, with something approaching awe It had been such a high spot in their lives that they spoke of it as if it had happened only last week; and it was a prized memory of important doings.

Yet, at the same time, it was a terrible memory of overpowering buildings, a nightmare of traffic and noise, that was forever coming into their thoughts and reminding them how lucky they were to live in this quiet place with the peace of the hills around them.

Their life-long seclusion had kept them fifty years behind their time, especially in their ideas about farming methods: Buster stubbornly resisted all kind friends who tried to persuade him to buy a little tractor, preferring to stick to his two horses however much food and care they needed. I could not help sympathizing with him there! The Harolds' manners, too, were old-fashioned, which made their rough, backwoods home, paradoxically, and oasis of gentle living in the midst of a crude modern world. Buster and Jessie were models of politeness, and so was their mother; I gathered that their father had been a ferocious old man when he had a mind to it, but in recent years he had mellowed down somewhat.

Although Jessie looked old-fashioned when she was dressed for town, she became almost modern at home, wearing a white shirt, a pair of light blue denim overalls, and a wide-brimmed hat for the sun; her hair seemed softer when it was untidy, her suntan looked good against the white shirt, and the blue of the denims brought out the blue of her eyes.

Buster had had every possible kind of awful accident and major operation, but seemed to be as strong as a horse: his father was immensely proud of him. "His real name is Paul," said the old man, "but Buster suits him better. He's always busting records. Hee! Hee! Hee!" I was horrified to learn, after Buster had carried me across the creek and back that day in the Canyon, that he had only one lung, and half his ribs were missing. One of his hands had been horribly mangled in the threshing machine, but he had refused to let them amputate it and, because he was Buster Harold and he willed it to heal, it had healed, and there were still plenty of jobs he could make it do. He was incredibly capable, and an extremely nice person. He had masses of curly, brown, greying hair, and a deep dimple in his chin. He was understanding and easy to get on with: the long periods he had had to spend in hospitals had made him more used to people than were the rest of his family.

It was a reward to know people like these, and to have my dream lake ringed with mountains – generous reward for all the hours of weeding and other dull jobs, and for the lack of baths and electricity, telephone, roads, and indoor sanitation.

The earth toilet, incidentally, was a very companionable affair, two in one, with a partition between. I shuddered to think how cold it must have been in winter, and how dark at night, and how trying the journey to it in the rain. For there were no holes cut in its doors for light and ventilation, and it stood beyond the hen-run, quite a trip from the house. Mrs. Harold used to refer to that trip only in hushed whispers, as "going along," and to the destination, not at all.

Pausing only for meals, I worked from half past six in the morning until at least eight at night. I did not consider this left me much spare time, but the Harolds worked far harder and longer than I. Though they were all up before seven (Buster rose at five or earlier) they were often busy until eleven at night: they made me feel almost idle.

Their three slow, restful meals were the only breaks the Harolds allowed themselves, and they certainly made the most of them. Jessie would lay the big, square table, spreading a white linen cloth over its heavy woollen cover and placing a bowl of flowers in the centre. She fetched plain white plates and jugs of creamy milk, and placed mats just so for the meat and vegetable dishes, and one for the teapot. When all the food was in, we stood while Dr. Harold said grace: "For what we are about to receive may the Lord make us truly thankful. Amen." Then the old man carved the meat, Jessie served the vegetables, and when everybody had his portion we all began.

I had never known anyone eat so slowly as the Harolds. Each day I took smaller mouthfuls, chewed them more thoroughly and paused longer between them, but still I finished my food long before the others. At the midday meal we always had the radio on, and as we ate we listened to the Harolds' favourite program, a serial story about a farming family not unlike themselves. But by the time Mrs. Harold had brought in the dessert and made the tea the program was usually over, and conversation would begin. The family sat for a long time over their tea and told story after story.

"You say you like your tea weak?" Buster asked me on the second day. "I wonder how you would have liked a cup the way Gustav made it?" He chuckled to himself.

"Tell her about that, Buzz," prompted Mrs. Harold. "Go on, do tell her."

"Didn't I tell you?" said Buster. "Funniest thing out, that was. There was this old-timer had a cabin way up beyond Deep Gorge. He was half Norwegian, or Swedish or something like that, and had a great, long beard. He was as nice as you could wish, well spoken and all that, but he'd been living up there in this little mouse hole of a cabin all alone for years, and I guess he'd got a bit queer.

"Anyways, Derek and I were up near there on a logging job, and one day he asked us in to tea. He goes out in the kitchen for a while, and then comes back and sets a great pot of tea on the table, and pours us out a cup each. I thought it looked pretty black when he was pouring it; but when I got mine, well, I could hardly get the spoon into it. Some tea!"

Buster screwed his face up and shook his head.

" Then old Gustav said: 'Guess I made it strongish today, do you mind it a bit strong?'

" We said that was okay; but I looked at Derek and he looked at me, and I asked the old man how much tea he did put in that pot.

" 'Oh, a fair lot,' he said.

" And I said: 'Yes, but how much?'

" Well, a pretty good lot. More than I usually put.'

" Yes, but how much actually did you put ?"

" 'Well,' he said, 'I guess I should have left out the last two hands full.' "

CHAPTER THIRTEEN

One of my favourite chores at the farm was putting the cows out every morning before breakfast. This is a typical morning: it is a quarter to eight, the milking is over, and breakfast looms pleasantly near. Although the sun is high and sunlight floods in through the wide door of the cow-barn, there is a sharp tang in the morning air, and I reach my jacket down from the nail over the milk-records and zip it on snugly. laden with full milk-pails, is already on his way to the separator.

Buster, " Buster!"

" Hello?"

" Shall I put the bossies out now?"

" Yes, if you like. Put them west, will you?"

" Right."

West, because we only send them east on days when we do not want to waste hours cow-hunting in the evening. To the west they have more choice of grazing places, and can travel further; eastwards, a mountain creek prevents them going more than a mile and a half along the lake shore. This business of sending them west, however, involves putting them across Harolds' own creek, a procedure which never failed to fascinate me the whole of the time I worked on the farm.

I unchain each little Jersey cow, quietly because they have been used only to these quiet, gentle people, but ruthlessly seeing that each one gets out of the barn at once: Buster feels he has enough chores without any broom-and-shovel work, and anyway I myself hate to tread in a cow-pat before breakfast.

" C'm on, bossies! C'sh, c'sh, c'sh. C'm on. Hurry on, there Daisy."

Gradually the little herd is persuaded to go down a trail between high wooden fences, and out through the big home-made gate with its tall headpiece onto the lake shore. I chase the last little heifer through, and, coming under the trees which border the farm, plunge suddenly into the full glory of the morning. The whole of the eastern sky is ablaze, and the lake is a lake of gleaming white light, rippling endlessly in from the distant mountains to the pebbles at my feet. Steep headlands drop to the water's edge at either side, silhouettes like cardboard scenery, with timber-jagged outlines: the nearest are almost black against the sun, the next less dark, and so on, each one fainter behind the brilliant haze until the furthest mountains can barely be picked out against the golden sky.

But this is no time to stand and stare: the cows, apparently from sheer cussedness, have immediately started in the wrong direction. Just what cows would do. I have to do a sheepdog's work, rushing up and down the pebbles, hopping on and off the huge driftwood logs to head them off. The dogs, of course, are in the kitchen waiting for their breakfast; their Union prevents them from working so early – for me, at any rate. But once the cows are resigned to going west there is no more trouble: they wander in single file behind the two boat-houses and along the pebbly shore under the trees.

Rounding the first bend we come in sight of the westward extension of the lake, another glorious view dominated by

Mount Ida in the distance. Here the creek comes rushing from under the trees to swirl into the lake, and separates us from the next part of the pebble path by at least fifteen yards. Any English cow, indeed, most Canadian ones, would turn back at this point, but not so the Harolds' cows. Oh, no. One by one they splash out into the icy water, heading apparently for middle of the lake. With very little encouragement from me they forge ahead, until at last they are in deep water, swimming for all the world as if it were as natural to them as grazing.

Nothing shows but their heads: pretty little horns curved upwards, and dark muzzles levelled to skim the surface. They travel in a great curve to avoid the creek's swiftest undercurrent, and come in again to the shore at the far side.

High water at the creek mouth. July 1950.

There is no sound save that of belaboured breathing, until the leader's feet touch ground and her bell comes above water. This first 'clonk' of a cow-bell emerging from water is an extraordinary sound: extraordinary in itself as well as in the fact that it is practically never heard. It is a kind of double "clonk", the first strange water-muffled note leading up in a weird scoop to the normal note, at least a full tone higher in the scale.

When the little herd is assembled once more on dry land there is no further need to wait; swimming is not so popular among them that they will enter the creek again without being driven. Nevertheless, I do wait, just for a few more precious minutes; for this is one of the few moments of the day which are entirely my own. A long, flat-topped headland – Orchard Bench – hides Salmon Arm from view, but over this towers my old friend Mount Ida, under whose lower slopes the little city is sheltered.

Salmon Arm.... To me, isolated over here, it represents all the joys of civilization: shops, cars, hot baths with bath mats and real taps, normal friends with normal ideas about life. Thinking of these things I am filled with nostalgia as I gaze across those nine miles of water and land; but then, I am filled with joy as I think of my freedom here from the dusty roads, the blaring jute-boxes in cafes, the paying of money for everything one does. Over there I could not sit on a golden, sandy point before breakfast, basking in a world of blue mountains, dazzling water, and ringing cow-bells!

Because it is these few minutes which make all the day's drudgery worthwhile, I prolong them by dawdling back along the shore. To my left is the barbed wire fence bordering the alfalfa meadow, to my right the lake. Between these the pebbly beach slopes down, shaded by spruce and birch, and strewn with huge, long driftwood logs. Now it is a wide slope, but as the lake raised with the melting snows it will narrow to a mere strip, crowded with logs, beside the fence. One year, Jessie told me, the water rose beyond the fence and she and Buster rowed the boat in and out between the trees.

Already the sun is getting hot, and enormous yellow and black Swallowtail butterflies are drinking on the damp gravel by the water's edge. The tiny waves come in, slap-slap-slap, always in a hurry. Ahead, beyond the farm, the mountain rises incredibly high and near, a great wall of spiked conifers growing almost directly above one another, higher and higher into the blue sky. One last look across the blinding water to the snowy mountains in the east, then I tear myself away and hurry up the front path, for it is after eight o'clock. Once more the barrier of trees hides the water and the distant hills. Once more, too, a welcome voice rings out:

"Oh Buzz. Oh Jess. Lavender. You kin come to breakfast now."

At five on Saturday afternoon I was waiting for Jessie. She had asked me to fetch the cows with her, so that I could learn where to go, and be able to do it for her sometimes. I did hope they would not be too far away tonight, for I was tired and stiff from hours of weeding, and it had been so long since lunch. Lunch, at twelve o'clock , was the main meal of the day; tea did not exist, and supper never happened until the cows were home and dry and the milking was all over. I supposed I should get used to it some day.

Here came Jessie, armed with a whistle hanging round her neck, a stick in her hand, and two excited dogs bouncing about her: time to go.

Cow-fetching only took an hour, and I loved the walk along the shore, in and out of warm, green clearings and the cool, scented shade of tall firs. Our feet were quiet on the pine-needles and on the grass; and the lake, shining between the trees, lapped softly on its stony beaches. If only we could have listened! But Jessie wanted to talk all the time, naturally she did. She had been alone so much, and she had done these long walks by herself day in, day out, for years and years. Of course it was wonderful for her to have company, and I must not mind her talking.

That evening was still and warm. Before I went to bed I walked along the beach to the creek mouth. There, I was alone to hear the night voices of the water and the woods; alone to see the lake lying at my feet; and alone to witness the strangeness of the mountains gazing up into the heart of the sky, and the sky gazing down into the heart of the mountains, silently, eternally.

CHAPTER FOURTEEN

Sunday counted as a day off. I was free to write letters in my cabin all morning, and Buster and Jessie were going to take me out fishing after lunch. Dish washing and milking chores had to go on as usual, but we did not even bring the cows in till after eight, and breakfast was not till nine. My, I was stiff! I had been bending over all Saturday morning putting ant-weevil powder round the roots of the strawberry plants, and I had been doubled up again all the afternoon weeding under the raspberries where the horse-hoe could not reach. I sat in the sun by my open door, nursing my stiffness, writing letters, and considering my position.

I had been at the Harolds' for three days. I liked the job, and I loved the place more every day, but I was not at all sure whether I should go on loving it for more than a few weeks, for it was so terribly cut off. The nearest place over land was the tiny village of Tappen, nine miles away, and that only accessible by two miles or so of game trails through the bush, followed by heaven knows what kind of road, with practically no traffic and certainly no buses. Canoe was three miles away across the water, and Salmon Arm was nine and a half miles which-ever way one went – via Canoe and the road, or round Merganser Point by boat. Supposing one could not get a boat and had to go round the shore by Tappen, it would have been a nineteen-mile journey. We had no telephone, and could only send or fetch mail when Jessie went over, every Thursday, to Canoe and Salmon Arm on the ferry.

I decided to stay till the end of June or early in July and just blissfully absorb everything, and get tough and suntanned and (I hoped) slim. Then, perhaps, I should go on down to the Coast, and eventually back home to England.

It was Sunday with a vengeance. Everybody had had a good wash and put on clean clothes, and the men had shaved. We lunched at the respectable hour of 1.15, eating in silence to the accompaniment of a broadcast church service. A radio is a great blessing when one is out in the backwoods; and at the Harolds' the reception was perfect, for there was no interference whatever. At breakfast, we had been able to hear a B.B.C. Broadcast from London: very nostalgic-making but at the same time comforting, for it shortened that six-thousand-mile gap for a while.

In the afternoon we were out fishing for three hours in the boat, and I had a chance to see more of the surrounding countryside. We went two or three miles down the lake towards Sicamous, going very slowly and trailing the three lines in the water all the way.

Buster caught a big Kamloops trout, and Jessie got two little fellows that they called Greys; but all I could catch was a piece of driftwood, and Buster's line under the boat. The sky and the mountains were much too impressive for me to be able to concentrate on fishing. From the middle of the lake one could see a long way to the east, where the peaks were bigger and snowier than the ones visible from the farm. A little storm blew up when we were on our way back, and the water turned grey and corrugated: we reeled in our lines, and went switch-backing home into the wind.

It was after six when we got home, but I went straight off cow-hunting with Jessie. We took two and a half hours over it, tracking and searching right up into the mountains away from the lake. I wondered: "Shall I ever learn my way around enough to go on these cow-hunts alone?" One had to know every single place where the cows liked to graze, and these were many but very far between. We had company on this trip – Dr. Holmes's two children Jill and Gordon, aged about twelve and ten. The Holmes family lived in Salmon Arm but had a lakeside holiday cabin a mile or so from the Harolds' farm, where they had just moved in for a fortnight.

It was very late when we got back, and the cows were wet from swimming the creek, so we had supper right away, while they dried off. I was milking by the light of an oil lamp till 10.0 p.m., and was still stiff from the weeding, but I was very happy. That night I had seen the two distant snow peaks glowing red when the sun went down, making a glory of colour up there above the sombre forests. The Alpengluhen, another of my old dreams come true!

CHAPTER FIFTEEN

More often than not the deep dimple in Buster's chin was camouflaged with beard like a pitfall with sticks and leaves; but when he had shaved and it was on view for a while, it used to fascinate me. At meal-times on a Monday or Tuesday my eyes would be drawn to it again and again. Such a round little hole it was, going so deep, right in! One day this dimple came up in a lunchtime conversation and I realized Buster was not in the least bit self-conscious about it.

" How do you manage to shave inside it?" I asked. " I've wondered so much. Isn't it rather difficult?"

" No, not very," he said. " Not with a proper cut-throat blade. If I had to use one of these fin nicking safety razors, though, I guess I'd jest have to shave right over the top of if and leave it all full of beard. I sure would look funny then, wouldn't I, Jes?"

" I guess you would, too," said Jessie. "Everybody's interested in that dimple of yours, and now its Lavender. Do you remember Gordon Holmes?"

Buster chuckled and turned to me. "You've met young Gordon, haven't you?" he said. "Nice kid.

When we first met the Holmeses, Gordon was only four or five, and not much higher than this table, but no shyness about him. They came to tea and the little fellow was sitting opposite me where you are now, and all through tea he stared at me. Didn't say a word, jest stared and stared and stared. Then after tea when we were showing them the garden, he came and stood in front of me and looked up at me, and he said: 'You have a little hole in your chin, Buster. What did you do, sleep on a collar-stud?'

Buster was not self-conscious about his hair, either, although it hung over his forehead in a great curly bush, and was long enough at the sides to cover his ears. "Haircuts are too darned expensive," he said. "I used to have one every two months, but the price has gone up and up; last time I went it was eighty cents. Eighty cents! I shall have it done twice a year now, and if it goes up any more I shan't have it done at all."

" I don't know why you never let me do it for you, Buzz," said Mrs. Harold. "Don't you think I make a good job of your Dad's?"

" Mother, I think you do it jest fine," said Buster, "but you have plenty enough work without doing my hair too. Anyway, I don't mind it getting long, and I can't see why anybody else should."

And nobody else did mind – except children. " I was over in Canoe once," Buster loved to tell people, "when I passed a man and a little boy on the sidewalk. The kiddy stared at me, and jest as I went by he clutched his father's hand and said 'Look, Daddy, is he a gorilla?'"

If Buster was innocently proud of his eccentricities, he was modest about his achievements. Jessie provided the praise due to her brother. "Buzz sure can build," she said. "He planned the cow-barn and hay-barn all himself, and he was the chief putter-upper, too. He has the cows in all the time in the winter, 'cos they can't get about in the snow and there's no grazing for them anyway. My goodness, then he's glad of his nice buildings. Aren't you, Buzz?"

" Don't know how we'd make out without them," said Buster.

" You should see how he works in the winter," continued Jessie. " He keeps paths clear from the north door to the hen-run and the cow-barn, and one down to the lake so the cows go down to drink. It sure is hard for him – isn't it, Buzz?"

" I wouldn't jest do it for fun," admitted Buster. " You know, Lavender, sometimes I've had to dig those same paths three or four times in a day, and half an hour after digging them more snow comes, so you wouldn't know there ever had been any paths. Some days we could do with somebody working full time jest shovelling snow."

" You'd find enough to do if you had another full-timer on the wood-chopping," said Jessie.

" Sure would."

" And then he does all the mucking out: cows, horses, bull, calves -"

" Hard work is the best way to keep a person warm," said Buster, and went off on some job.

" One of my winter jobs," said Jessie, " is to take the cows down to the lake to drink, twice every day. That's not a warming job! Smashing up the ice for them is okay, but standing around waiting for them all to drink – brrr!"

" I don't know how you stand the winter here, year after year," I said.

"I should hate it."

" Oh, it isn't so bad. There's no chores in the garden, and no fetching the cows off the mountain in the evening. That's one thing we like about the winter, chores are all over early and we get the nice long evenings to sit in and read, and sew, and listen to music on the radio. We feel we are really people of leisure then."

Winter 1949-50 @ Herald's Farm   Looking down the front path at the frozen lake ,   Photo by Buster

Leisure – they pronounced it "leesure" - was tremendously prized by the Harolds who had so little of it. Forever busy, there was nothing they longed for so much as a little free time: time to relax, time to absorb the peace of their surroundings, time to do the countless little jobs that had had to be put off day after day and week after week. Perhaps – who knew? - one day they would even have time enough to unearth their treasures and use them every day.

How they did love showing me those treasures! Treasures put away and never used, because the family had so little "leesure", or because "the old shack's no fit place to have them out"; treasure put away but dearly loved and never forgotten, always being brought out and shown fondly to admiring visitors such as myself.

There was a glass-fronted cupboard full of pretty china, and a box of good silver locked away. Jessie showed me her very own cup and saucer, given to her by a friend some years before, but still kept wrapped in tissue paper in the box in which it had first arrived. She had never drunk from the cup. When she had showed it to me, she put the box back in the chest of drawers in her mother's bedroom, and brought out another box for my inspection. This last was a leather case containing an expensive propelling pencil, which had been sent to her the previous Christmas by another friend. Jessie hardly ever had the occasion or the desire to write anything, but even so, the propelling pencil was her own and gave her immense pleasure.

The piano was another treasure. It was piled high with copies of Reader's Digest and stiff in some of its keys, but deeply revered nevertheless. " It is a hundred years old," said Mrs. Harold with pride. " It's a real good piano, that." She was sad, and a little ashamed, that it had not been tuned for almost two years. "But we can't afford such luxuries," she said, " when we're not using it at all. Jessie has no time for that sort of thing now, the work is too much for her."

" But that's a shame," I said.

" Jess used to play a lot, she was quite good," said Mrs Harold. "She took some lessons years ago. She ought to play for you. Jess!"

" Yes, Mother?"

" Jess, why don't you play something on the piano so as Lavender can hear you? You used to play so nicely."

But Jessie refused on account of the piano being out of tune and herself out of practice. I was sorry, for her musical bent interested me, and I longed to hear her perform. One day she opened a leather case and showed me the very apple of her eye, a guitar wrapped carefully in silken rags. She had had it for five years now. She had saved up for years to buy it with her own money, then she had taught herself to play it, and used to entertain the family with it in the long winter evenings. But now, alas, one of the strings was broken, there had been no time to bother with getting a new one, so she could not play it for me.

There was considerable artistic talent in the family. Once Jessie showed me several sets of floral china, all hand decorated by her mother. There were cups with cascades of purple violets, leaf- clad saucers, and plates with delicate wild roses; none of them very original in design, perhaps, but the workmanship was perfect and the colours exquisite. I was amazed; and even more so when I saw Mrs. Harold's paintings

Jessie persuaded her mother to bring these out of their drawer and show them to me herself. Together they propped the big portfolio up on a chair, and Mrs. Harold placed each picture on the table as Jessie handed it to her. A country scene with fruit trees and a wagon of hay; a flower group; two or three more landscapes; and a great many more flower compositions, some in water colour and some in oils. The pile on the table grew slowly thicker. Jessie was silent and expressionless as she handed out the pictures, and her mother was full of modest explanations and apologies as she laid them before me, but around them both the very air was warm with pride and joy.

The landscapes were mediocre, and interested me only in their subject matter – prairie farms in summer, looking surprisingly like English scenes. But the flower paintings amazed me with their beauty – beauty of colour, of composition, of technique; these were all good stuff. I had had no idea I was working for an artist. Mrs. Harold told me casually that painting and china decoration had been her chief occupations on the prairie before she had married. I was horrified that hands – and brains - capable of such work should have been dedicated year in, year out to a lifetime of the most arduous menial chores; and I could not help but show my feelings. Why, here was an artist married to a doctor, and for all these years one of them had been wasting talents which might have given joy to thousands, and the other had neglected a hard-won skill which might have lived and grown and proved of value to all humanity.

Neither they nor their offspring, however, appeared to have any regrets about wasted talents. Buster, while recovering from one of his many accidents, had once won an inter-hospital drawing competition of over a thousand entries. His picture, a landscape beautifully drawn in pencil, hung on the living-room wall; it was the only drawing he had ever made. " I jest can't see what all the fuss was about," he said when I admired it. "There's nothing to it, nothing to it at all."

" But Buster," I cried, " you should have been an artist! If you could do that with no teaching or even practice, just think what you could do if you went in for it seriously!"

" That's what other people have said," he complained. " 'You ought to be an artist.' Why should I? Why? I don't want to be an artist! Drawing and painting should stay where they belong, as spare-time hobbies. I'm farming: now that's something worthwhile."

CHAPTER SIXTEEN

Mail for me, mail at last! I had been at the Harolds exactly a week. Thursday had come round again, and with it the ferry-boat taking Jessie off in the morning to Salmon Arm and bringing her back, together with the week's shopping, a pile of newspapers and a bunch of letters, in the evening. "Plenty of mail for you," said Jessie.

Nobody – unless he has been far away from all his friends in a place where he could only send or receive letters once a week – nobody can imagine how much that meant to me. Every week when the boat came in I used to feel like a shipwrecked man on a desert island sighting a distant ship; and if it brought nothing for me, I felt as though rescue had been denied me.

There was nothing from England this time; but a mysterious parcel had come, a long letter from my sister in Ontario and, amazingly, a charming letter from Den. He had found lodgings and started work at the hospital, and sounded happy; but his letter contained more questions than news. He begged me to write and tell him about my new job. " Had a letter from Mother," he wrote, "and she says you are going over to Harolds' for a month. I am just curious to know why you chose them?"

I was unreasonably thrilled at hearing from him, and told myself as much; but when I opened the parcel I had reason enough for pleasure. It, too, came from Den, though he had not mentioned it in his letter. Inside were the two nature books he had recommended to me, one on mammals and the other on trees, shrubs and flowers.. A brief note was enclosed: " Thought you might find these useful. They are an un- birthday present. Hope you see your chipmunk soon."

A present! They were first-class books, beautifully illustrated and packed with information, yet small enough to carry around easily: exactly what I had longed for.

I liked them so much that I would gladly have spent my own few precious dollars on them, and they must have been expensive. But a present.... I did not know whether to laugh or cry.

I had known chipmunks would be enchanting! It was the day after the books came from Den that I saw my first one, down on the shore. Jessie pointed him out to me, else I should never have seen him, so quiet he was, and so grey on his grey driftwood log.

We were scrambling over the rocks of the East shore, the cows hurrying home well ahead of us, when Jessie suddenly stopped dead. " Lavender," she whispered, "Come here, very quietly." I came.

" There's a chipmunk on that log. Can you see him?"

" No."

She pulled me in front of her. " That big log with the sticking-up end. He's near the right-hand end. See him now?" " Oh, Jessie, I can't."

I was afraid it was going to be another failure, as when Den had tried to show me one. All I could see was a perfectly ordinary, grey old log. Perhaps chipmunks were invisible to me?

Then exactly where I had been looking there was a jerky little movement, and there he was, as visible as anybody else. He was soft and furry and very small, but there was a bold gleam in his round, dark eye. He clung to the log, legs bent ready for action, white tummy touching the wood. His furry tail was resting along the log behind him; it was as long as his whole body, but not big and bushy like the tails of his squirrel relatives. I admired the brown and white bands along his sides, and the same pattern in reverse on his face: he was very attractive.

Suddenly it seemed as if he remembered something. He dashed along the log carrying his long tail straight and high over his back like a kitten's. But when he had gone only twelve inches or so he stopped to gaze out at the lake. Then he inspected the wood between his front paws, looked sharply about him, sat down to scratch, and got up again. Everything he did was in sudden jerks, and every jerk was accompanied by a flick of his ridiculous tail, up high, out straight, curved over his head, up high again, always so stiff for its absurd catstail length.

Jessie and I exchanged smiles, and went on watching. The chipmunk, quite unaware of our presence, ran down onto the pebbles, round to the back of his log, and up on top of it again. There he sat up straight and ate something in a tremendous hurry, holding it in his two front paws and chewing so fast that it made my jaws ache to look at him. When he dropped down onto all fours again, Jessie said we had better go on. As we moved, one pebble clinked against another, and the chipmunk vanished in horror. I never saw where he went.

Searching in one of my beautiful new books (H.E. Anthony's Field book of North American Mammals) for further information about my chipmunk, I found to my astonishment that he was one of no less than seventy species: Charleston Mountain Chipmunk, Cliff Chipmunk; Least, Long-eared, Redtail and Yellow Pine chipmunks – chipmunks of every description. "There is," says Anthony, " scarcely any peculiar ecological association in western North America which does not have its own peculiar form of Chipmunk, provided the animal can find food there."

Thumbing my way through pages of descriptions, and inspecting rows of pictures, each one of a prettier animal than the last, I tracked down my friend and found him to be the Gray-headed Chipmunk, the very same whose enchanting pencil portraits in Driftwood Valley had captured my heart two months before. I judged him to be the prettiest of the whole lot, with his bright eyes, gay stripes, and neat little figure: he is only eight inches long, and half of that is tail.

I found out that all Chipmunks, unlike the tree squirrels, make their nests underground or in holes in rocks and do very little ,climbing. I read that they tame easily and make interesting pets; that they have about five young in a litter; and that they are subject to parasites. Pity about the parasites: I should have loved a pet chipmunk!

I also found from this fascinating book that the food of the chipmunk consists chiefly of nuts and seeds, berries and buds, which he stuffs into his cheeks and carries to his burrow "sometimes with such a quantity in the side of the face as to cause a very obvious swelling." Just like a child with a huge sweet! Alas for the chipmunk, sometimes he unknowingly eats forbidden sweets, and then it is the worse for him. In mid-June Buster shot a gopher and a chipmunk. He brought the chipmunk to my cabin, thinking I would like to see it, but I could have cried. He explained why they must be shot, by pushing his forefinger into its cheeks and bringing out about a dessertspoonful of unchewed grain.

I understood, but I was sorry all the same. I took the little fellow and propped him up in a sitting position against a box and tried to sketch him, because he was so beautiful; but his vivacious charm was gone forever and my drawing was as unlike a real chipmunk as was the little corpse before me. So easily do we destroy beauty.

The gopher is another non-climbing relative of the tree squirrel; in fact, one of its more formal names is Ground Squirrel. There were plenty around Shuswap Lake, living in colonies in all the clearings. It was a long time before I saw one properly, but during the evening cow-hunts I was always hearing their piercing whistles coming from beyond the trees before I reached a clearing.

At the first warning of anyone approaching they would set up an earsplitting din of shrill whistles, which they repeated again and again, pee, pee, pee, peee, until the danger was past, or until it grew bad enough for them to have to pop into their burrows. The sound fairly rang through the woods, and it didn't seem as if it could possibly be coming from furry animals, it was more like the call of some strange bird – most of all like a boy whistling with his two fingers stuck in his mouth.

The dogs could never resist the temptation. One whistle, and they would be gone like a couple of torpedoes, ears flapping, pine-needles flying up behind them - no time even to bark. Not that barking was necessary: the noise of snapping twigs, thundering feet, and frantic, fortissimo panting was enough to scare any gopher out of his wits.

The single alarm note grew to a whole chorus of whistling, then suddenly there was silence, as if they had been switched off. When I reached the clearing a few moments later, there were two foolish-looking dogs, but never a gopher to be seen; they were all safe in their burrows. The dogs had never been known to catch one.

There was only one place where the dogs could not prevent me seeing the gophers, and that was the meadow beyond the Cookes' house, a mile away to the west of the Harolds. In case there was trouble with Cooke's dog I always used to put Patch and Blackie on leads in that neighbourhood, and we were way up the path above the clearing by the time I let them loose again. The colony down in the meadow set up such a whistling that the dogs were nearly frantic and it was all I could do to hold them. But the gophers didn't always vanish into their holes, and from up on the path I could often see them, sitting up stiffly like so many tent-pegs in the grass. I longed to get a close view of them, but didn't get a chance until I had been with the Harolds almost a month. It was the last day of June, and overpoweringly hot. I was feeling tired and not a little sorry for myself, for I had spent all morning doing some form of depressing drudgery in the kitchen, and two solid hours doubled over picking strawberries in the heat of the afternoon sun. I went early for the cows, and for some reason or other did not take the dogs with me.

For once I heard the bells as I rounded the first point of the shore, and found the cows grazing their way homewards just beyond the Harolds' boundary fence, only a quarter of an hour's walk from home. I brought them in through the prairie gate (an ingenious and economic contraption made of three strands of barbed wire and a movable fence-post) and took them across Larch Point, on the Harolds' uncleared land. On the way I heard the gophers whistling up in the little pasture, and it suddenly occurred to me that now would be a good time to go and stalk them. The cows were well ahead of me, and now I had them safely within the boundary fence there was no need to see them right home; also, having fetched them in less than half the usual time, I felt justified in taking the next half-hour off for my own purposes.

I left the path and tiptoed up cautiously through the trees, careful not to step on any twigs. The whistling continued, and I went very slowly, stopping every few steps, until I was near the pasture.

That pasture was a favourite place of mine. It was only about an acre in size, a lovely, round, green acre filled with sunshine and guarded by tall conifers. It was a friendly place: there were spruce-cones and spider webs and wild strawberries in the grass; and in the late evenings, when the horses loved to graze there, heavy feet and mysterious munchings were to be heard, and round rumps, pricked ears and white blazes loomed through the gathering darkness. Buster had only cleared the land a few years before, and had "always been meaning" to clear at least as much again, if only he had had time. I knew he needed the extra grazing, but I loved the pasture exactly the size it was.

The grassy patch, for all its dips and hummocks, was level compared with the sloping woodland around it, and below it the ground dropped steeply for a few yards, forming an earth bank which was covered with a dense thicket of young cedars. I crept under the feathery green branches, wormed my way up the bank on my front, and surveyed the grass from gopher's-eye level.

At first I could see nothing. There was less whistling going on, and I was afraid most of the gophers had gone underground. I lay still for a while and listened: there seemed to be only two or three animals calling now, with less anxious calls than before. "Too many hummocks in the way," I thought. I inched forward away from the dead leaves and twigs out onto the quieter grass, and, as the whistling still continued, raised myself very slowly and carefully to a crouching position.

Instantly there was silence, and two, three, four little brown forms moved in the grass, and were gone, flick! flick! flick! Before I could even see what they were.

I was cursing my clumsiness, and already preparing to get up and go home, when pee, pee, pee! rang out loud and clear, and I saw a gopher straight opposite me, no more than a dozen feet away. It was sitting bolt upright, ridiculously long and stiff, like a little stump or stick. "What a perfect camouflage!" I thought. "It is exactly like that small stick beside it." Its yellowy-grey body was long, nearly a foot long; but there were only few inches of its bushy tail. Its front was a bright, buffy colour, and I could just see its beady eyes.

All at once I realized that the little stick beside it was no stick, but a baby gopher, sitting stiffly upright just like Mother. Then as if by magic there appeared a second baby, as vertical and as motionless as the first. Pee, pee, pee, called the mother, twitching her short tail nervously at each call; and something small and brown ran through the grass and joined the group. Pee! Peeee! Soon I counted four babies; but evidently the mother gopher, too, could count, and four was not the right number for her. Again and again she called, and at last a fifth little fellow appeared from nowhere and sat up obediently beside the rest. Now the mother seemed satisfied, and gave only a warning note now and again.

I could hardly believe my luck: I wondered if Buster and Jessie had ever seen a gopher family like this. There they were, all in a row facing me; Mrs. Gopher with one baby on one side of her and four on the other. Five very small stumps and a bigger stump, and the bigger stump letting off a piercing whistle every few moments.

I stared, and they stared, until at last I had to move. Then, on the instant, silence, and where there had been stumps there were puffs of dust, five little puffs and a big puff. I never saw them move. I went home laughing to myself, all self-pity forgotten.

CHAPTER SEVENTEEN

Buster told me I was to have a holiday on the Sunday, going back to civilisation. He said I could have Saturday evening off too, because there were no buses from Canoe on Sundays. He promised to take me to Canoe in the boat, but even so, he said, one could not bank on catching any particular bus on the other side: one could never be sure of the weather, terrific storms whipped up suddenly and the lake became quite dangerous. However, I was hoping for the best. I planned to stay at the hotel on the Saturday night, have a paradise of a real bath, and see something of the Meeks on Sunday. Then, I supposed, I should have to walk those six and a half miles back to Canoe, hoping to find Buster waiting there in the boat. Talk about backwoods!

It was grand to have the prospect of a whole day off, for that week I had been growing more and more tired. On Wednesday morning I had slept through the noise of my alarm clock for the first time, and Jessie had had to come and wake me at a quarter to seven. The same thing had happened next morning; and on Friday I was so weary that when I went over to my cabin after lunch I slept for an hour by mistake, instead of writing letters.

The weather may have had something to do with it, for it had been muggy and thundery, and towards the end of the week it was hot enough to work in a sun-bra for the first time. But I think that what tired me out far more than the weather was a dreadful thing called a wheel-hoe. This is an implement consisting of a small wheel, two horizontal pieces of metal designed to slide under the weeds, and a pair of handles. You hold the handles and push the thing in front of you; pull it back a little and push again; and push, and push, and push, till you come to the end of the row. It astonished me how exhausting this occupation could be.

Buster introduced me to it on Tuesday afternoon, and told me to do between the sugar beets. These were grown for winter feeding for the livestock: Buster had planted seventeen rows of them, all at least two wheel-hoe widths apart, and every row so long that it took me ten minutes to get along it, working fast. I wheel-hoed all Tuesday afternoon, most of Wednesday, and all day Thursday. After the sugar beets I did the turnips, and after turnips I did the carrots. Then the beets and the radishes. The rows seemed to get longer and longer; I was wheel-hoeing all Friday and part of Saturday, with blisters on my hands and a stiffness in my shoulders, but with a great determination to get it finished.

At eleven o'clock on Saturday morning I came triumphantly to the end of the last row; but almost immediately I was sorry, for there was no more garden work just then, and I was degraded to house work in the form of ironing. Ironing took place in the alley-way, and had to be done with two heavy black flat-irons heated on the top of the stove. Jessie had been at it since breakfast and was glad to hand over for awhile. The day before, she had spent the entire day doing four weeks' accumulated washing, and the amount of ironing to be done was quite fantastic.

Aprons, cotton dresses, overalls, and slips. Trousers, long underpants, bush shirts, and handkerchiefs. Sheets, pillowcases, and tablecloths. My own bluejeans. Endless ironing! I worked at it, getting more hot and sticky every minute, from eleven till twelve, then again for two hours in the afternoon, and still there was some left for Jessie to finish. I envied Buster, working outside on the site of the new house: he had ploughed it on Thursday, and now he had Duke harnessed to the big iron earth-scoop, and was beginning to dig out the hole for the foundations.

However, even four days of wheel-hoeing and three hours of ironing were not without their compensations. Twice that week I had been allowed the honour of fetching the cows for Jessie on my own. I had walked quietly, listening to the sounds of the forest, and loving the way the soft-coloured cows walked single-file before me through the sunshine and the shade; I had seen my first bald-headed eagle, also more squirrels, and another chipmunck; and I had begun to find wild strawberries in the clearings. On Thursday there had been the thrill of getting letters, and those wonderful books from Den; and on Wednesday night there had been the music.

There was a concert on the radio in the evening, and everything was re-organised on that account. When the cows came home they were left in the meadow, where they had to wait while we rushed through supper and dish washing and then sat back to listen to our music. Until that evening I had not known that the Harolds appreciated music. This was only a light concert, but the way they loved it sent them up yet further in my estimation. Everybody listened in complete peace, complete relaxation, no-one spoke, no-one knitted or read. We listened to the entire first act of a Gilbert and Sullivan opera before going out to finish work, and it was well after ten when Buster and I started milking.

Saturday evening came at last. I knocked off ironing to got and fetch the cows early. They had gone east and were not very far away, but not very co-operative either: just this day of all days they chose to keep dashing off into the bush in the wrong direction, and I had to do a lot of running. Blackie the spaniel followed at my heels, like the dear, useless little thing she was; while Patch, who was old and wise, and who worked well for Jessie but not at all for me, just sat and smiled tolerantly. When at last the homeward procession got going in its usual order (old cows, young heifers, Patch, myself, then Blackie) it went so slowly that I began to lose hope of ever getting to Salmon Arm. You just cannot hurry cows.

But I managed it. I put the cows in the meadow at half past five, did a lightening change and bolted my supper, and Buster and Jessie and I were away in the boat by six. Luckily the bus was comfortably late. Buster and Jessie came into the village and waited with me, to see me off.

The "bus", when it came, turned out to be just an ordinary old car, none too big, driven by a young man in a brightly checked shirt. If he could not fit all his prospective passengers in, why, they just had to wait while he drove into Salmon Arm and came back to make a second journey for them. But this time everybody fitted in. There were three or four people in the front beside the driver, and at least seven in the back, all sitting on top of one another. I was in the front, squeezed tightly against the door, praying it would not burst open. It cost fifty cents to travel like this, but it was worth it to avoid the walk.

I went straight to the hotel, checked in for one night, and found myself with my same old bedroom. The first thing I did was to ring Mrs. Meek, but I am afraid she must have found me exasperating: one thought was running in my mind, one thought alone.

" What are you going to do -" she began.

" I'm going to have a BATH," I cut in, visualizing the two taps turned full on. " I mean what are your plans, while you're over here?"

" Well, before I do anything else at all I shall go up and have a bath -"

" Yes, but when you've had your bath?" She was getting impatient, and no wonder. In the end she managed to get it over to me that she wanted to invite me up next day, and we arranged that I should ring her at ten in the morning.

That bath was magnificent – a whole bathroom to myself, with a door that locked, and a clean floor with a bath-mat on it! A big white bath-tub, and shiny taps with hot and cold water streaming out of them, as much as ever I wanted! Hot water without kettles seemed miracle enough; but best of all was having a bath-tub I could sit right down in – that was the height of luxury. I sat there in a blissful trance with the warm water wrapping me round, and washed and soaked, soaked and washed, revelling in everything, even the small convenience of a sponge-rack.

I was unbelievably dirty, but even when I had washed it all off, my back and arms were a deep golden brown. When I stood up in the water I could see them in the mirror, and I had a delicious self- admiration session. It was the first time I had seen the suntan on my back, for the mirror in my cabin at the Harolds' hung high on a beam, and was so small I could only just see my face in it.

A big rough towel and plenty of talcum powder completed my orgy of civilized cleanliness, and when I came out I felt intoxicated with the freshness and sweetness and luxury.

I spent all the next day, Sunday, lazing around. I was completely clean, completely idle, and completely happy. Mr. and Mrs. Meek were kindness itself. They fetched me at midday and would not hear of my leaving until it was time to go to Canoe, where they drove me down in the car to meet Buster and Jessie: I need not have worried about the six-and-a-half-mile walk, after all. Mrs. Meek lent me her bicycle to explore the lanes in the afternoon. She gave me lunch and tea (real English tea, with bread and butter and cakes, at four o-clock!) and supper.

We sat on the verandah in the shade, and there was time to read, time to talk, time to do nothing at all. It was a perfect day for doing nothing: 90 degrees in the shade, our hottest day yet. Mr. Meek snored gently in an armchair. I read magazines, dipped into books, and chose a book to borrow.

When I admired the two photographs on the piano, of Den looking outrageously handsome in Air Force uniform, Mrs. Meek brought out an old album and showed me all her snapshots of him from babyhood upwards. He was her adored only child, she missed him very much and loved to talk about him. "He's a dear, funny boy," she said. "In a way I think he has never grown up at all – all this craze for expeditions into the bush. But he is sincere through and through, and I think that is terribly important, don't you?"

We talked on about Den; we indulged in reminiscences of England; and I told her about my life at the Harolds'. Finally we discussed the exciting possibilities Vancouver held for me.

" Do you think I might get a temporary job as a waitress there?" I asked, hungry for new

experiences, and imagining the fun of telling the family about it afterwards.

" Surely you could," said Mr. Meek, waking suddenly. "All the students take jobs like that in the summer, it's the thing to do."

" I'd like to do something of the kind," I said. " It would be an experience, and it would pay for a week or two's stay there. I want to see Vancouver properly, and I'd like to look up one or two people I met on the train."

I thought of Mrs. Hope's dear old mother whom I had met a Sicamous, and who had been so charming to me in those few minutes. I should call on her, and on the girl Janet. I should look up some old friends of my own family, I had their address.

" Den might show you round a bit," said Mrs. Meek.

" Oh, that would be wonderful! Might he show me round the University?" " He'd love to, I know."

" And I'll see the Pacific, really and truly the Pacific Ocean?"

" As good as. There's Vancouver Island in the way, and what you'll see will be Georgia Strait really. But an island hardly counts, even a big one. After all, it must be Pacific water all round it."

" I wonder what I'll think of Vancouver? Everyone told me Toronto was wonderful, but I hated it!"

" You won't hate Vancouver. The mountains are so close; you only have to look down any street and there they are, towering over you."

" I'm getting quite excited about it already!"

" You will have all sorts of fun there. I wish I could be going."

Mrs. Meek loved the Coast dearly, and was very keen that I should go there.

"When you have come all those three thousand miles across Canada," she said, " it would seem a pity not to go the other three hundred and see the Coast."

It would have seemed a pity, indeed.

We discussed the matter thoroughly, and I decided definitely not to stay over with the Harolds after the end of June. When I left, maybe I should stay in Salmon Arm for a week or two, thinning fruit in the Meeks' orchard (Mr. Meek's own suggestion); then I should go to Vancouver, and perhaps on to Vancouver Island. I might get a fruit-picking job on the Island, or come back to the Interior and get one in the Okanagan Valley. I did want a job with more free time, and with possibilities of meeting more people, either during or after work. I realized this need even more acutely now that I had had a day away from the Harolds' farm. But for another two and a half weeks I could be very happy as I was.

On Monday it was as hot as ever, and before lunch I had my first swim in the lake. I resolved to do so every day from then on: it was wonderfully refreshing, and quite made up for the lack of baths.

After supper I broke it to Mrs. Harold and Jessie about leaving. It was a miserable and difficult business, for they were openly distressed by my announcement; they badly needed the help, and pleaded with me to stay. I felt very selfish, but I had to be hard-hearted. I compromised a little and told them I would stay five weeks: mentally, I fixed the outside limit at six weeks, which would mean leaving not later that July 15th.

Buster received the news far better, and took me off to show me how to work the engine for the separator.

CHAPTER EIGHTEEN

Mid-June brought summer weather such as I had never known, and I wanted it to go on for ever. Temperatures soared into the nineties day after day with no sign of change; I continued to swim in the lake every day, a necessary habit as well as a pleasant one. I used to swelter along endless rows of vegetables with a hoe, getting browner and browner but, extraordinarily enough, no slimmer.

I was growing fond of my family Harold and, perversely, now that I had fixed a date for leaving the farm I found more and more happiness there. I loved the peace in which I could think matters over while I worked; I was fascinated by the wild life around me, and I used to work up a positively childish excitement about my weekly mail; but my chief joy was the overwhelming wonder at the scenery. My efforts to describe it in letters home only resulted in fruitless long periods of staring through the trees at sparkling, rippling, swish-swishing lake water and hazy blue mountain shapes, during which time my pen-nib dried up. I knew I could convey nothing of it in a sketch, and it defied all thoughts of poetry, for it was already a poem. " If you can think of the loveliest stretches of water you have known," I wrote in one letter, "in every mood that water takes on, and the biggest, grandest, wildest and most peaceful woods, and the hottest summers; and if you can combine all these with wooded mountains and snow peaks, you have perhaps an inkling of the kind of enchantment I walk in all day."

As for the wild life, I saw more of it, and learnt more about it, every day. " If you happen to meet a porcupine," said Mrs. Harold, " jest you keep well clear of him. When a porky gets frightened he'll swing round at you with his tail, and if that hits you it leaves quills sticking in."

" Nasty things, those porky quills," said Buster. " Do you remember poor Rolly, Jes?"

" Poor old Rolly!" Jessie turned to me. " Rolly was a shepherd dog I had years ago, before Patch," she said. " He was a dear dog, and intelligent about most things, but jest plain stupid about porcupines. He'd a quill in his nose two or three times. Most dogs will touch a porky once and never again, but not so Rolly: I guess he wanted to have his revenge. It sure took a lot to teach him his lesson.

" One day I had taken him out after the cows when he ran off the trail into the bush. I heard him barking, and he paid no attention when I blew the whistle. Then there was a scuffling noise and a terrible whimpering, and I found him whining and shaking his head and rolling in the leaves. He had hundreds of quills stuck all over his face, some of them right through his muzzle so he couldn't open his mouth. I think we counted two hundred, didn't we, Buzz?"

" Two hundred and seven," said Buster. " Jes took every one of those quills out."

" It took me two hours," said Jessie, "and that was one very unhappy dog for a week after. But it was the last time he tried anything out on a porky."

Buster told me fascinating facts and stories about other animals and birds: one day he told me how the humming birds sometimes hitch-hiked their way up to British Columbia from the south, hiding under the feathers of the big northward-flying geese. Once he and Jessie showed me the single footprint, five inches across, of a cougar, or mountain lion. The print, in a muddy patch in the meadow, was so big and had impressed them so much that they had marked it with a stick and had preserved it for a year.

I hoped I should never meet its owner! Cougars, I was told, have a nasty habit of lying quietly along branches all day, ready to drop on you when you walk underneath. I just tried not to think about cougars at all, for bears were about as much as I could stand.

Buster was braver than I. " You aren't scared of a poor little bear, are you, Lavender?" said he. " But you needn't be: he's much more scared than you are. Why, I've frightened a bear without much trouble. Haven't I Mother?"

" Eh? Oh, yes, sure. Sure he has, Lavender." Mrs. Harold's eyes twinkled. " Tell Lavender about that, Buzz."

" It was last summer," said Buster. " I'd been out after supper to have a last look at the irrigation, and it was getting dark. On my way back through the garden I noticed something queer about a certain bush. I thought, ' That's a very dark shadow under that bush.' I was curious to know what it was, so I crept very, very quietly a little closer, and a little closer. I felt almost sure it was a bear; then I heard him grunting and snorting and I knew. When I was about as close to him as I am now to that door, I stopped and kept very, very still, trying to see him. He was grunting and sniffing and snuffling in there but he didn't come out. I got another step close, and I could see his back moving.

" Then I felt a darned sneeze coming, and I held my breath and tried to stop it, but it had to come. I made it as little a sneeze as I could, tsnew! But it was too much for the bear. That bear came out of his bush and went jest as fast as any darned thing I've ever seen, lickety-split across the meadow and into the trees, and I could hear him running up the hill for quite a time after. All 'cos of one little sneeze."

" Now you know how to scare the bears off, Lavender." said Mrs. Harold.

" Just sneeze," said Buster. "You shouldn't ever need to worry about bears, with your hay fever!"

However, on those long evening treks on the lake shore and up the mountains in search of cows, I did think of bears, always. I used to frighten myself over them. I wonder, do other people frighten themselves too? It is all too easy. One starts with some apparently harmless thought, a chance spark of the imagination: just for fun, one lets the spark catch, then the small flame of thought is so fascinating that one watches it, fanning forgetfully until it is suddenly a dangerous fire which must be beaten out.

I remember letting this happen to me one hot summer morning in London. I was looking into a little shop window when a man came out of the shop and brushed the back of his hand against my bare arm for an instant as he passed. Though I scarcely saw him I sensed that his touch was intentional, and walked off, withdrawn and defensive. I was uncomfortably aware of him staring after me. I could still feel the place on my arm where he had touched me, and a sudden thought flashed into my mind: supposing he were a leper?

The thought grew: I pictured a sinister, evil leper – no, a suffering, jealous leper, grown cruel in his bitterness and wanting to inflict his own horrible disease on anybody young and healthy like myself. The spot on my arm seemed to burn into my flesh, and I dared not touch it with my other hand for fear of spreading the infection.

I even began to plan how I would wash it with Dettol as soon as I got home. But perhaps disinfectant would be useless against leprosy? Leprosy! Fear crept into the pit of my stomach. But as I turned the corner at the end of the street, safely out of sight of the shop and the man, I was able to make myself come down to earth, quenching the silly fantasy before it became a real terror.

Some months later I casually related the incident to a friend, and thought for a moment she was serious when she suggested I should come as a patient to the mental hospital where she worked: it is impossible to say exactly where sanity merges into insanity.

In the bush I used to get similarly worked up, thinking of bears. As I stepped quietly along beneath lofty hemlock trees, listening for distant bells and searching for cow-tracks in the dust between the pine-needles, I used to be as alert as a corned-up horse on a frosty morning, with every sense awake and receptive. Like a horse I would find myself looking for things to shy at. A mouse in the dead leaves, or a dry twig snapping underfoot, would be enough to send me side- stepping, with wide eyes and a delicious thrill of fear, across the path; the curse of a squirrel in a suddenly swaying branch would be enough to freeze me in my tracks.

Now I knew exactly how horses felt when they shied. I knew, too, how quickly their little excitements could grow to big terrors. One or two half-intentional shies, and my pulse would quicken. A few more, and, with my heart thumping within my ribs, I would begin on a line of thought something like this: "I am afraid: why, when I am used to being alone in the woods? Must be because of the animals, wild animals that are new to me: coyotes, wolves, cougars, bears. Yes, bears.

Because of owls and eagles and snakes too, but chiefly because of bears. Supposing I saw one now, what should I do?

That tree over there looks branchy enough for me to climb, I'd run for that. I wonder if the bear would climb too? Perhaps it would be better to run down into the lake. My God! What's that?" A rustling footstep, a grunting noise, and a black furry shape beyond some bushes! I felt my hair rising on my scalp and my knees stiffening; but after an eternal split second I realized I was staring at an old, charred tree-stump. I had heard only a robin moving in the dead leaves, and one of the dogs snuffing behind me.

After that, every black stump would be a potential bear, until the fear grew so big that I had to be firm with myself, or I should have had to run home without finding the cows, which would have been foolish and cowardly, as well as very annoying for the Harolds. "You mustn't think about bears," I said to myself. "You mustn't anticipate them, it doesn't help." So in due course the stumps would become stumps again, and the small sounds of the bush would cease to startle me; and soon I would come upon the gentle cows and busy myself about driving them home.

But one day I actually did meet a black bear. It was on Tuesday, June 13th. The cows had gone west; I had been searching for them in vain for two hours and was a long way up the "logging road" above the top of the canyon. Following a minute path which Jessie had taken the time the Holmes children had come with us, I came pushing out through the branches into a wide, level place, clear of undergrowth but shaded with immensely tall, old spruce trees. I wandered away from the little trail, searching for cow-tracks and straining my ears for the sound of a bell.

But everywhere the straight columns of the spruces stood silent; there was no sound but the pattering of the dogs' feet beside me, and the faint roaring of the falls in the canyon far behind. I took a few steps forward, and stopped to listen again; then I saw him.

He was behind a tree-trunk about thirty yards away; I could see the front half of him silhouetted blackly against the pine-needle dusk of the woods, and I particularly noticed his tufty, rounded ears. He did not move. Black bears, everybody had told me, were harmless - "unless," people would add darkly, "you meet a mother one with cubs, and happen to go between her and the cubs." When one meets a bear, how is one to know it is not a mother one, and that her cubs are not hidden on the wrong side of the path one is about to take?

For a moment I had the strange sensation of observing my own reactions quite impersonally: "Shall I be afraid, or shall I not mind at all?" I wondered. The bear and I stared at each other for fully thirty seconds without moving, then suddenly I knew I was afraid, dreadfully afraid. But on no account must I let the bear sense my fear. Luckily old Patch was beside me. I put my hand down and put him on a string, never taking my eyes off the bear: somehow I felt that Patch might protect me if I kept him close beside me. Still the bear stared and did not move. Then I turned deliberately and walked away, trying to look casual and unhurried, never looking round until I came back to the end of the level ground and had gone downhill enough to be out of sight. Then I ran. Although I had been exhausted after a long, hot day, I found enough energy to run down an awful lot of mountainside, through wild forest, fast. I ran for about ten minutes, coming, as Bust would have said, "lickety-split down the mountain," until I came to the lake shore.

There was a big, stripy snake on the stones, and I saw my second eagle at close range; but I had had such a scare that I cared nothing for them. When I had satisfied myself that the bear had not followed me, I sat down to get my breath, while Patch and Blackie splashed into the water to cool themselves. Poor Patch, he looked puzzled and hurt and tired. I was hot and clammy, and a bit shaky: I decided I had had as much as I could take, and would go home without those cows, even if it meant getting the sack.

When I got home after eight o'clock, humble and guilty and worried about my reception, I found to my amazement that the cows had just arrived before me, having crossed the creek above the canyon top and come racing down the mountain north of the farm.

Nobody was cross, everybody sympathized about the bear, and life went on as usual. But I did hate going west for the cows, after that.

CHAPTER NINETEEN

Mixed bathing was not the order of the day at the Harolds'. When Buster bathed he bathed alone, and everybody kept discreetly away. Everybody, that is, except myself. I went to my cabin, but I couldn't resist peeping out of the window.

Buster went into the boat-house with a bundle under his arm, and was in there for at least five minutes. Every few moments I looked down towards the lake, and there was no sign of him. Then a door banged, and I saw an extraordinary figure wading into the lake. It was buster all right, I could tell by the hair; but his bathing-suit was a heavenly Victorian affair, all loose and baggy, with sleeves nearly to the elbows and trouser-legs to the knees. It was so decent that it was almost polo-necked, and to crown all it was an excruciating shade of purple. It must surely have belonged to his great- grandmother. It was odd enough to embarrass anybody, but what embarrassed Buster was not so much that he was too prudishly covered as that he was showing an indecent amount of leg. I realized how very tolerant he had been about my working in a sun- bra: it must have confused him at first. He had professed to be worried about my getting sunburned, but had been unable to look at me while saying so.

Once a young couple came to lunch, the woman wearing the briefest possible green shorts. After the visitors had gone and we were all congregated in the kitchen, Jessie said: "Did you ever see such funny little shorts?" Buster was silent a moment, his bushy brown eyebrows indicating horror at what the world was coming to these days. Then his eyes twinkled, and he said: "So they were shorts, were they? I should have called them no-see-ums." "No-see-ums" is the name the Indians have for midges.

If Buster disapproved of bodies appearing in a state of nature, he felt differently about faces. He expressed much the same views as Den on the subject of make-up.

Whereas Den had said: "I like a girl to be so you can pour a bucket of cold water over her and she still looks as good;"

Buster said: "I can't bear women who smear a lot of paint on their faces so you wouldn't know they were faces at all. Bah! Making their lips bright red, and their nails as if they had been in at a pig-killing. I jest can't make out why they think they look better that way."

Although I could not always agree with Buster's ideas about fashion, I did like his attitude towards animals, and towards the little things that can mean so much but often go unseen. There was the time when he met my bumble bee. The bumble bee lived in the roof of my cabin, between the beams and the thick paper that was nailed up there for a ceiling. The paper ended a few feet from the door, but the bumble bee lived over the head of my bed, I could hear her moving about up there. In the early mornings there would be a papery rattling and scrabbling, enough noise for a large mouse at least. Then a buzzing and rustling would travel invisibly above the paper, away towards the door, and suddenly, boom, out would come Mrs. Bumblebee. She would blunder about the room and crawl up and down the window in a state of frustration, wanting to get to the delphiniums which were only a few inches away. When the summer nights grew warmer I used to leave the door open, and then she would always fly straight out in the morning and go round to the flowers. I always had the door open in the daytime, and while I sat writing letters after lunch the bee would buzz in and out every few minutes, going under the paper at the same place each time, and rustling along until she was directly over my pillow. When she got in there, she was always very busy.

Something important was going on. One day, after a couple of weeks of this mysterious work, the early morning booming seemed louder, and when I got up I found no less than three bees on the window, in spite of a closed door. I had no doubt now as to what had made my bumble bee so busy.

Although I never had any particular affection for her children, I grew fonder and fonder of Mrs. Bumblebee, and was glad she had helpers now. I told Mrs. Harold about her, and when she suggested destroying the nest I would not hear of such a thing; but I was relieved to find that the bee family was not increasing any further.

One afternoon I was resting on my bed and expecting Buster to come and use the post-drill for something. At length I heard him coming across the lawn, and at the same time I heard my bumble bee moving above the ceiling away from her nest. She boomed out at the end just as Buster was asking if he might come in; as he crossed the threshold the bee bumped into him and buzzed crossly away, thrown out of her usual pathway. For a split second I was afraid he would be angry and slap at her, perhaps even come remove her nest in mistaken kindness to me. But I should have known Buster better than that: his good manners were an integral part of him, and he was unfailingly polite.

"Hullo, Bumblebee," he said gently, and stepped aside. And I felt all warm inside, as one does feel when two of one's friends meet for the first time and like each other at once.

CHAPTER TWENTY

It had been thundery all the week. Today, Thursday, the temperature had been up to 99 degrees, and I had been thinning beets and weeding carrots. I wore as little as ever, forgetting that all my previous suntan had been acquired in an upright position. Whenever I bent over, my jeans dragged down to expose an extra inch of flesh, and by the end of the afternoon I had a fearful red band of sunburn across my back. Now I should have to be careful how I lay at night.

But I almost forgot the heat and the sunburn, for when Jessie came back from Salmon Arm she brought me no less than four wonderful letters, and one of them was from Den. " I'm glad you like the 'wild-and-woolly-West' " he wrote. " I can just see you carrying milk-pails in your blue- jeans!" He told me he was going to inquire about fruit-picking jobs from friends on the Island, also, perhaps, about other work in Vancouver. " Ring me up when you come," he said. " If I have an afternoon off we can get a car and go for a drive around. I know you'd love it here, it really is beautiful with the sea and the mountains."

After I had read my mail I longed to be alone with thoughts I could not share; I slipped away at dusk and walked eastwards along the shore. It was very quiet. I met a toad on a rock; I found the nest (a mere hollow among the pebbles) of my favourite pair of sandpipers; and once a fish jumped high out of the lake and fell back with a plop! into the smooth, dark water.

Round the first point, out of sight of the farm, I sat down on a log to watch the darkness deepening over the lake. The stars were coming out, and the night air was warm; there was no sound save the infrequent plops of fish, no movement save that of the spreading ripples.

Then the train came. First, the deep whistle murmured faintly in the east, and vanished into silence; then it sounded again, nearer, echoing from mountain to mountain up the lake, wild and thrilling. Far away, a light winked at the foot of a mountain, was gone, winked below a nearer mountain, and was gone again. Then, at the end of a headland, there was the light moving, and another light – a long band of light sliding along the shore. A faint roaring came across the water, and the whistle blew again; the band of light broke, re-formed and broke again, passing in and out of the cuttings in the rock. Three or four times it vanished altogether, but always it reappeared at the tip of another headland, each time a little larger; and the roaring grew louder and louder.

This was the same train that I had come on, exactly three weeks before. As I watched the band of light tracing the dark shore-line I thought of Sicamous, of Den, and of the last ecstatic lap of that long journey.

The bright streak became a row of lights, and the row of lights became a row of coaches with individual windows; I gazed across the mile-wide lake at it, wondering at the passing of those three weeks, wondering that I could be on the far shore beneath the woods, watching the train, no longer inside the train watching the far shore.

Then it had gone past, and the separate lighted windows merged once more into a single, luminous streak, trailing away towards the west. Soon it would be stopping at Canoe, then Salmon Arm, then it would go north to Marten, and west again down to the Coast. Soon I should travel on that train myself! Maybe I would go on a Thursday again, so that I should feel it was truly the same train as before; and I would continue on from Salmon Arm and complete the journey to the Pacific Ocean.

The thread of light moved away, joining the nostalgia of the past to the hopes of the future: as I picked my way home among the logs and stones of the shore, I watched it vanish round the last visible point, and my thoughts leapt ahead to Vancouver and the Coast, and to the things I would do there.

Below the gate I paused for one more look at the quiet, brooding mountains, and at the wavelets bobbing on the shingle. Suddenly a great call rang out across the lake, and my heart missed a beat. The loon! Again it came, wild, oh, wild beyond all belief; a cry from the very soul of all untrod lands and waters. A deepened curlew-call, it was, a post-horn fanfare, thrilling, echoing, yet with the soft quality of wood-wind. There!

And again! And each time, the faint, wild echo was tossed up from the far shores and lost on the air.

Then came such an outpouring of weird laughter that I shuddered in the warm night. It was vibrant, mirthless, incomprehensible. Was this the maniac cry that gave the bird its American name? One could imagine a lunatic laughing this under the moon. Three times it burst forth, then died away and left the taut air shaking with its memory.

The loon, the Great Northern Diver.... This summer land of timber and water must have seemed tame, almost cozy, to him who knew the ice and rock wastes of the North. This land, so vast and wild to me, made a fitting enough background for his voice; but what of that other world?

I imagined those clear trumpet calls ringing through the Arctic night and echoing from berg to berg; I imagined that laughter dancing in the frozen air and setting the Northern Lights themselves a-shimmer. Then I felt humble about my little journey to the civilized West, and saluted the winged travellers with my heart.

I went to bed inexplicably happy because I had heard that weird and desolate call of the loon upon the water – a strange eloquence, distilling into one phrase all the wildness of this great, wild land.

CHAPTER TWENTY-ONE

At the week-end it was sill blazing hot. The snow was melting on the far mountains, swelling the rivers and making our lake rise faster and faster. Every day the water crept further up the beaches; by Saturday morning, alas and alack, it had submerged my poor sandpipers' nest.

While the heat caused the rivers to flood and the lakes to fill up, it dried the land to hard, cracked lumps and fine dust. Buster had let the water into the irrigation ditches in the field, and from these into tiny temporary ditches running between the rows of plants in the garden. The water was plentiful, for it all came from the big creek in the Canyon, along a level, open ditch which contoured the mountainside above the fields, just up under the trees. At intervals, smaller ditches left this level ditch at right angles and ran down into the field; Buster dammed or cleared the head of each, according to his needs.

A great deal of minor damming and un-damming was going on at the top end of the all-but-level garden, where a complicated system of little irrigation ditches began. These were hardly more than furrows: Buster had made them by driving Duke up and down between the rows with the horse-hoe, to which he had fixed a special ditching attachment something like a miniature ridging-plough. Now he spent hours attending to the dams, sometimes letting the water flow down one group of ditches, sometimes down another. On Saturday he left me in charge of all these waterworks while he cut hay in the front meadow: I found it a full-time job. The little temporary dams needed constant attention; and I had to puddle up and down the rows with a special kind of hand hoe, removing blockages, and pressing down the soil in places where the water had seeped away through cracks and left great lengths of ditch quite dry. I was delighted that all this playing with water should be counted as work.

Sunday was my day off. We did not milk until after eight in the morning, and there were no chores for me after breakfast. Although Buster and Jessie went off in the boat for the day, I chose to stay around the farm. I wrote letters in the morning, washed my hair, and did very little else all day.

I walked out to the point by the creek mouth and lazed the afternoon away there alone, reading and dozing, sunbathing for a few minutes at a time then retreating under the trees from the fierce heat.

On my way back I stopped at an old bonfire site, now half covered by the rising lake, where the gravel was charred and blackened and mixed with a fine dust of ashes. I stopped to watch a butterfly I had seen. It was a Swallowtail, its wings spread to catch the sunshine and its proboscis busy on the damp gravel. I kept still and looked down at the beautiful patterns on its wings, yellow and blue and black, with a row of ruby spots along the hinder edge. Even as I looked I saw there was another one beside it, and another, and another. Ten big Swallowtails I counted, all within eighteen inches of my feet, and I had not noticed them! I would not have believed it possible that such brilliant markings could merge so perfectly into a background of charred gravel.

I was cleaning shoes in my cabin later when I heard an angry chattering in the trees down by the beach. From my doorway I could see a squirrel scrambling and leaping through the branches at a great height, and, one tree behind him, another in hot pursuit, cursing volubly all the time. They were jumping from tree to tree, up and down, now hidden behind the leaves, now reappearing further along. The angry one did not seem to be gaining on his victim at all: the two of them were still one tree apart when I lost sight of them and their scolding died away into the distance. I hoped the fugitive got away. I liked the local variety of squirrel. They were as small as the English red ones, but their coats were grey-brown and ticked like those of wild rabbits, and they all had clean white shirt-fronts.

That evening Buster and Jessie were home in time for milking and supper. Jessie had bought a new sheepdog bitch from some people further down the lake shore, and brought her back in the boat. She seemed to be a nice, gentle little thing. Jessie wanted to train her to take Patch's place, for he was old now, and tired easily. She decided to call this new one Tess. " I like to give them short names, easy to call," she said.

At sunset Buster and Jessie went off again in the boat to visit the Lesters, our "next door neighbours" who lived more than a mile away across the bay. I stayed at home for I wanted to finish this quiet, unhurried day alone and go to bed early for once. By ten o'clock I was lying in bed reading by the light of my Aladdin lamp, which was balanced precariously on a pile of books on the chair. Before Buster and Jessie had gone, I had had my first "Harold bath" - a remarkable experience. I would not have missed it for the world, but I did not want to go through it again: I preferred to stick to my daily dip in the lake.

The trouble was the amount of preparation which seemed to be necessary. Special big pots of water had to be set on the stove beforehand; and, while they were heating up,

Jessie fussed around getting things ready. She took a tin tub upstairs and set it on the floor of Buster's room, clearing all Buster's things away from near it. Then she produced an odd-shaped bucket from somewhere, a tall affair with a tap at the bottom and one flat side for hanging against a wall.

When the water was hot we poured it into this bucket and carried it upstairs. Jessie hung it up on a beam in the roof above the tub, and fixed a rubber tube onto the tap. The tube had a spray at the end, and a gadget for shutting the water off just behind the spray. Jessie showed me at great length how to work it, gave me a clean bath towel and plenty of last-minute advice, and finally left me alone. "Call me when you've finished," she said as she went down the narrow stairs, "and I'll help you carry the tub down."

I undressed and stepped into the tub. I turned the water on barely log enough to wet myself and my sponge, then made the sponge very soapy and washed all over with it in one go. A second economic spraying was only just enough to get the soap off, but it was good to feel it streaming down my body, warm and clean. I did not attempt to sit down, because there was too little water to slosh over me, and in any case I should not have fitted in, even with my knees tight against my chest.

Drops were scattered around on the rough wooden floor, and I knew some must be falling through between the boards, for I remembered them coming sizzling onto the little stove in the sitting-room once when Jessie had been bathing.

I dried and dressed very quickly, for the stairs came straight up into Buster's room without any door, and I was afraid Buster might not know I was having a bath in his bedroom.

I carried the tub downstairs alone easily, emptied it on the garden, and made a second journey for my wash- things and dirty clothes; I left the odd-shaped bucket for Jessie to deal with. Now I knew why the Harolds did not take a bath more often than once a week.

CHAPTER TWENTY-TWO

When I had turned out my lamp and settled down for the night, there would always come a solitary mosquito buzzing around my pillow. If there were several I would re-light the lamp and swat them all (so I thought) out of existence. But no sooner was I ready for sleep again than the thin, high-pitched whine would begin, faintly at first and then coming in a horrid crescendo right up to my ear, ee-ee. Just one. I think I would have preferred a whole swarm. I used to pull the sheet up over my head, hold it down so tightly over the pillow that hardly a germ could have reached me, and wait till the mosquito seemed to have gone away. But within two minutes of my emerging again it would be singing round my head: ee-ee-ee.

Maddening! Sometimes it got caught in my hair and buzzed on an even higher note until it was free. On these occasions I could slap at my own head until it ached without ever hitting the mosquito. If I lit the lamp, my tormentor would merely vanish until I turned it out again. On most nights I admitted defeat and fell stuffily asleep with the sheet still over my head.

I used to dread scratching mosquito-bites in my sleep. My legs were permanently covered in them, and there were always several on my arms and body. I scarcely noticed them during the day, but towards evening they would begin to itch. Jessie lent me a bottle of lotion but its effects were short-lived. Of course, the best cure would have been to avoid scratching, but once I was asleep I lost all control. Time after time I used to wake up in the middle of the night, huddled far down under the bedclothes with my knees pulled up to my chest, rubbing and rubbing at my legs.

The irritation was so intense that I knew I must have been rubbing and scratching in my sleep for a long time. And, short of tying my extremities to the four corners of the bed, what could I have done about that? I soon learnt to accept mosquitoes as a normal part of life, and itchy bites as a normal part of my body.

Fortunately, insect life on Shuswap Lake was not entirely aggressive; some manifestations of it fascinated me. For instance, there were extraordinary insects in the kitchen – wasps of some kind, with very long waists. They looked much the same as ordinary wasps when they were at rest, for their folded wings covered these long waists; but when they were flying, well - First the main part of the insect would come past, and then way behind it there was the rest of it, like a trailer on a long tow-rope.

The first time I saw one I thought there must be something wrong with me, and tried to forget it quickly. But a day or two later another one zoomed past and nearly hit my face while I was drying dishes; after that I often saw them, and always in that particular corner of the kitchen. They flew in and out of the window in a most business-like fashion, and I learnt to keep clear of their usual route. When I asked Jessie about them, she said : " Oh, I expect those are the mud-daubers." We went to the kitchen and at once she found something on the closed half of the window. "I guess these are the ones you mean, aren't they?"

"Why, yes, so they are."

There were two insects walking slowly about on the glass, their abdomens palpitating with their breathing – a kind of remote-control breathing at the end of those tubular waists. They were black with yellowish markings and yellow legs; I had not noticed the legs before.

"Yes, those are mud-daubers," said Jessie. "Have you never seen them before? Well, there's another new Canadian thing for you! We've got plenty of mud-daubers in Canada. They build the cutest little mud nests, but we get fed up because they will build them in the house. They've been building in the soap box every summer for years; I had to give it to them in the end, 'cos there didn't seem to be any way to stop them. I have to keep the soap in the cupboard in the living-room now. Little nuisances they are!" She pointed out a big old soap carton on top of the kitchen cupboard, and sure enough, as we looked a mud-dauber buzzed out from behind it and sailed down and away through the window.

"You can't see the nests from down here," said Jessie. "They're all round the back, or inside. I'll get Buster to lift it down and show you tonight; then they will all be sleepy and won't mind so much."

At bed-time that night Buster lifted the box gently down and brought it near the lamp. "Well, Lavender, here are your little mud houses, do you want to see them? Only a peep, now, or they will wake up in the light, and we don't want you getting stung."

Buster half opened the battered old box, and when I peered in I could see three untidy blobs of hard clay, I was surprised at how small they were: none of them measured more than two inches across. I asked Buster if they made them any bigger, but he said no, these were the finished articles.

"They are not like ordinary wasps," he said, climbing on a chair and sliding the carton back into the exact position it had been in before. "They only have five or six grubs in each nest."

He got down and put the chair away. "Five or six grubs," he repeated, "side by side, each in a tight little bedroom an inch long. Those houses may not be much to look at outside, but they are mighty cleverly made inside."

"Buster takes them out in winter when the owners have finished with them" explained Jessie. "Then we can look inside. I wish we could show you, Lavender. Don't you wish we could, Buzz?"

"I do," said Buster. "You sure would like to see them, Lavender. And you'd never guess what the mother mud-dauber feeds her children on."

"Honey? Flies? Caterpillars?" I suggested.

"No, none of those. Spiders. I've smoked the mud-daubers out in summertime when they did their building in awkward places, and then I've opened up nests with the grubs inside. Each grub was shut in with a big, fat spider for food. Clever little beasts: they sting their spiders just enough to paralyse them but not kill them, then they shut up one in each cell, and an egg with it. When the maggot hatches out of the egg he has enough food to last him till he's grown up. Sometimes I reckon if we were as clever as insects we'd get along okay.

CHAPTER TWENTY-THREE

I lay in bed listening to an early humming-bird zooming and whistling up in the lilac bush. Sunday's laziness had done me good; for once I was awake early, and need not get up for a long while yet. When I did rise there would be the milking, the walk along the shore to put the cows across the creek, then, a long way into the future, there would be breakfast.

I had become used to a light breakfast now, for dinner was always large and very early. I was allowed, thank, goodness, to have cornflakes instead of porridge: two big helpings of cornflakes with creamy milk followed by toast which Jessie and I made for ourselves, going out into the kitchen in the middle of breakfast to do it.

On my first morning I had eaten my plateful of porridge, hating it all the time. The second morning I had attacked it with all the will in the world and far greater appetite than the day before, but it had sickened me so that I could not finish it. I laid down my spoon and admitted to Mrs. Harold, though I had never intended to do so, that I should simply have to eat some other kind of breakfast.

Buster used to laugh at my cornflakes and swear he could "never do a morning's work on such little bits of paper." He himself had nothing but porridge, and said he did not know any other food which would last him until noon.

Buster sat opposite to me at table, and it never ceased to fascinate me to watch him eating porridge. He used to have two full-sized soup plates of it, one before him and a second waiting beside him. Each was filled right over the flat, outer rim, the porridge coming within a quarter of an inch of the edge. Buster, like the rest of his family, ate incredibly slowly, but very steadily. When he had salted his porridge carefully he would begin by eating small spoonfuls from the left-hand edge, until there was a little trough around that edge. Next he would lay down his spoon, take the milk-jug and fill the little trough with the rich, yellow milk. This done, he would enlarge the trough, taking milk with each spoonful until there was none left, when he would lay his spoon down again and pour on a little more. With slow, steady concentration he would continue in this way, eating, adding milk, and eating again, until he had worked his way right across the plate and finished every scrap of porridge so that you would hardly know the plate had not been washed. Then, keeping his spoon, he would put the empty plate on one side, draw the full one towards him, and begin all over again.

That Monday morning I finished all the weeding, and strenuously helped Buster to move some enormous logs; after lunch I worked in the hay with Jessie for two hours, in a stupor of heat and sweat and hay fever. It was a relief to go and fetch the cows with her, crossing the creek and walking westwards under the cool trees, and stopping to eat wild strawberries in the clearings. The hay harvest was in full swing, and David Birmingham had come over to help Buster for the day. I was glad to meet David at last, for I had heard much about him. His mother – who spent every summer in her cabin on the shore a couple of miles away – was very friendly with the Harolds, and used often to call in on a Sunday for a can of milk.

David was like her, sun-tanned and freckled, with twinkling brown eyes, and dark hair bleached by the sun. He was also tall and slim and young; I found it refreshing to have someone new here, most especially someone young.

But why, oh why did I so often have to meet new people when my eyes were streaming with hay fever, and my nose sore and shiny, and my face perpetually buried in a handkerchief? It was sickening. I was not much affected by alfalfa, which, fortunately, formed the greater part of the Harolds' hay crop; but what Jessie and I had been working in that day was ordinary meadow hay. I stuck at it, for in spite of the sneezes I preferred it to housework.

We were putting the hay up into cocks -at least, I should have called them cocks, but the Harolds called the coils. There seemed to be no end to the new words and expressions I was learning in British Columbia: jugs were called "pitchers," loose boxes "box stalls," market gardens "truck gardens," and cart-horses "work-horses." When Buster referred to his "boison berries" in the raspberry patch I thought at first that he said "poison berries," and wondered why he let them grow there; it was a long time before I realized they were a kind of edible fruit I had not come across.

Perhaps the oddest word I had so far met was "stone-boat." That one puzzled me very much at first. One afternoon, the washing-up over, I escaped into the sunshine and went looking for Buster. He was up at the end of the meadow working with one of the horses, and I walked out to him, through the vegetable garden, under the apple-trees, and along the narrow path between tall grasses.

He was unhitching the horse when I reached him, and he had not seen me. " Hello, Buster," I said.

He looked up and smiled. "Hello Lavender. I didn't know you were there, creeping up so quietly. All finished in the house now?"

" Mm. Anything I can do for you now?"

" C'm on Duke. Whoa -whoa, now. Yes, Lavender."

I concentrated hard for the coming instructions: Buster spoke so softly I often found it hard to understand him. I did not like to ask him to repeat things too much, for that seemed rude; and in any case he never raised his voice, even for the repetition. When Buster spoke it was as if he were coaxing a very small and timid kitten, or soothing a frightened colt.

"Yes, Lavender," he was saying. "You can take Duke, if you will, and go and fetch the stone-boat and bring it out to me here. It's just by the hen-run."

"Right."

I picked up the long reins, which were lying, Canadian fashion, on the ground behind the horse's heels.

"Come on, then, Duke."

I drove Duke off down the path in the hot sunshine, steering him carefully round the edge of the garden, avoiding both the freshly dug earth on the right and the tall alfalfa on the left. I hoped I looked efficient, for I certainly did not feel it.

What on earth had Buster meant? Stone-boat: it did not sound remotely like anything I had ever heard of. Surely I must have heard him wrongly? Evidently it must be something a horse could pull. Wagon? Mowing-machine? Sledge? Hay-rake? No, not the hay-rake, that needed two horses. Perhaps it was not something horse-drawn, perhaps he had meant me to put Duke away and fetch it myself. I began to panic. It was too late to turn back and ask, I had almost reached the farm buildings.

I searched all round the hen-run and found only the big sledge, nothing else that I could have imagined Buster wanting in the meadow. I hitched Duke to it, got on board and drove out to the meadow.

To my relief, Buster did not appear puzzled or irritated.

"Is this what you wanted?"

"Yes, thank you, Lavender, that's right."

Praise be! But I had to get this thing straight. "Buster," I said, "do you know, I thought you told me to get the stone-boat!" "I did."

"What a funny name!"

"Is it? It is kind of like a boat, and it goes along over the stones, I guess."

David left on Monday evening while we were still having supper, and went back in his little rowboat to the cabin. He had promised to come again on Tuesday: Buster would start carting then, "if the weather held." Surely it would. Even the nights were warm now. I had taken my cabin window out and propped it against the wall behind the chair. Soon I should be able to sleep with the door wide open.

On Tuesday I thinned sugar beet all day long. It was still stiflingly hot, but Buster had been right to mistrust the weather. In the afternoon the thunder-storms came at last, with a wind swaying the trees and driving the showers before it. Once the breeze dropped and the rain came roaring down for half an hour, flattening the plants, making the dust into mud, driving us all into the alley way and showing up several furious leaks in the kitchen roof.

Buster and David brought in several loads of hay before the showers began, and once Buster fetched me away from my sugar beets for a while so that I could watch the way the hay was unloaded into the barn. It was all done by pulley, a whole load at a time. Buster laid a large rope net on the floor of his wagon before loading, and did not make his loads very high. When the wagon was full enough it was brought close under the barn wall; the two ends of the net were pulled out from the front and back of the wagon, and handed to the man on top of the load (usually Buster) who drew them together and hooked them onto the end of a long rope. This rope went up over two pulleys inside the barn roof and down again to the ground, where a pile of its loops and coils lay idle.

When Buster had fixed the net he jumped off the wagon and unhitched the two horses, and David hooked the free end of the rope to the tripple-tree behind them. When all was ready David led the team down the track towards the lake; as they strained forward the net on the wagon was drawn tight, and the whole load was pulled up into the air. It swung against a steep wooden ramp on the barn wall and travelled slowly up it.

By the time it reached the entrance at the top, David and the horses were right down on the beach.

Buster shouted to them to stop, for now the huge net of hay was sliding clumsily over the top of the ramp to hang directly under the first pulley. At this moment the clip which fastened the ends of the net together was automatically released, and the entire load dropped into the barn. Now the horses were brought back and hitched to the wagon, somebody went up a ladder to catch hold of the hanging net and pull it down, and it was placed back on the wagon ready for the next load.

That was all – no pitching up at all, and Buster was able to spread the hay about inside the barn at any time that suited him.

Buster and his brother had designed and built that barn themselves, ramp and all, not to mention the cow-barn beside it. The hay-barn was an enormous timber building, wide and long and with a high roof. Inside, with its flat roof half as high as the barn eaves, and its floor down below the ground, was the root-store. This had thick walls and an underground tunnel entrance with two doors: the innermost door was thick, heavy and close-fitting like the door of a safe. By the time the harvest was in there was a great thickness of hay packed all round and on top of the root store, forming a perfect insulation.

In the heart of his winter's hay store Buster kept his winter's supply of swedes, sugar beet and giant carrots, safe against the hardest of frosts and the deepest of snows. One entered the tunnel from a sheltered alley way which also opened on the cow-barn, the calf stable and the yard: over this alleyway the hay-barn communicated with the cow-barn loft, where there was a hole in the floor over each hay-rack. Winter feeding was made as easy as possible in such buildings, and no hay or roots needed ever to be carried through the snow outside. The mucking out was easy too, for the alleyway was wide enough to accommodate an entire season's muck-heap and still leave room for the cows to come by on their way in and out.

"Guess I'd soon be an old crock," Buster said, "if I had to plod through feet deep of snow every day, wheeling manure and toting hay for all the cows and horses. And I couldn't dig any more paths than I do."

It was strange to think, in that scorching weather, of the long months of snow and ice and bitter cold against which the Harold brothers had planned their outbuildings. It was strange to think of the deep snow covering everything, of Buster digging paths to the hen-run, the barns, the lake, and the bleak and distant toilet; strange to think of Jessie taking the cows down to the lake every day and breaking the ice so they might drink.

The hen run in winter @ Herald's Farm ,Photo by Buster

When the ice was thick enough on the lake, Buster and Jessie could pull a toboggan across on shopping days; but often it was thin, or there was only a fringe of it round the shores, just enough to prevent transport by boat, and in such conditions they were completely cut off. Even when the toboggan could be used, the snow upon the ice was sometimes so deep that progress was almost impossible, and in blinding blizzards Buster and Jessie themselves had more than once been lost for hours out on the open lake.

The Harolds accepted the difficulties and terrors of their life without question, without thought of complaint. Theirs was a greater happiness, a deeper contentment than I had ever seen in the more sheltered world I came from. But even so, I had no wish to spend a winter over at the farm myself.

I spent a second whole day thinning the sugar beets, but still they were not finished. Mrs. Harold told me to save some of the thinnings for her to cook for lunch, and they made a delicious dish of greens.

It had been rainy, off and on, and thundery sometimes. The lake was still rising fast, and the beaches were getting so narrow that it was often difficult to get the cows past the jumbles of driftwood. Sometimes they had to swim out into the water while I scrambled over the logs, and sometimes we all had to make a detour inland between the trees.

Because of the rain there was no haymaking that day, but David turned up never the less. He came to the cow-barn at eight-thirty in the evening, and engaged me in a lively and ridiculous battle of wits while I milked; we both enjoyed ourselves immensely. David was like a tonic to me here.

The next day, Thursday, I went to town. The only work I did was milking and helping Buster load two squealing, pink pigs into crates to go on the ferry for selling. It was a very sociable day for me. David was on the boat, and he and Jessie introduced me to the other passengers, who were all "neighbours" of the Harolds by virtue of their living on the lake shore, although their homes were miles apart. Among them were two charming French-Swiss women, who begged Jessie to bring me along in the boat to visit them on Sunday.

In Salmon Arm David took me out to lunch and then on to visit an aunt of his. Later, I went to see Mrs. Meek in what she called her "office," and told her about the wonderful books Den had sent; she said he was job-hunting for me in Vancouver. How kind everybody was!

Before I saw Mrs. Meek I had another glorious hot bath in the hotel. She found these baths of mine amusing, but I myself considered them absolutely necessary. The Harolds, too, thought me a bit odd, for I always insisted on washing my feet before going to bed. Each night I brought a basin and towel and slippers into the kitchen. The lamp was lit and everyone was friendly and sleepy. Jessie was brushing down her long hair, and Buster was collecting the various pieces of the separator to assemble them ready for the morning milking; the old Doctor had gone to bed, and Mrs. Harold was just sitting on a stool talking, ready for bed but unable to tear herself away from the conversation.

I squeezed myself into a corner between the table and the cupboard, put my bowl of hot water on the floor, and washed both feet and then both socks. I had to work at top speed, for the warm kitchen was full of mosquitoes which rushed for my bare, wet legs and bit mercilessly: the Harolds found the whole performance tremendously entertaining, especially the mosquito-slapping and the squeals and complaints which accompanied it. But it was worth it, to go to bed with clean feet.

CHAPTER TWENTY-FOUR

When he was younger Dr. Harold's life must have been work, work, sheer physical work, with no time for hobbies. His work was itself his pleasure. When I knew him he was an old man, pottering about and sitting on a chair at the edge of the meadow watching his son bringing in the harvest. "Lavender," he used to say, "this is the first year I haven't helped in the hay myself."

When he was not watching the harvest, he was watching the lake. He used to sit on a log down on the beach for hours and hours just watching, and he knew the "put-put" of every boat. When a boat was nothing but a speck in the distance, he would listen to the particular "put-put" of its engine and say: "Here comes Derek," or "That must be old Garlick." He loved that lake as much as he had loved it when he gave up his career to live on its shore.

Sometimes I wondered whether he had been justified in imposing his way of life on his young family. He was much talked about in the "civilization" which was Salmon Arm, and not always favourably. His children had grown up without even seeing a church or a school, or a city.

Although they had none of the things modern civilization has to offer, they were unconscious of any lack. But was this right? Should they not have had access to the amenities their father chose to ignore? Should he have imposed his own unusual choice on growing children? Often I was inclined to think "No," especially when I thought of poor Jessie and her beard.

I soon got to know that Jessie and her mother both shaved, and that when pressure of work delayed such refinements the older woman grew only a few white whiskers, while her daughter developed dark and prickly shadows on her chin. But it was not until I had been at the farm almost a month that I heard the story of Jessie's trouble.

David had taken me to visit his Aunt Edith in Salmon Arm, and Aunt Edith and I began talking about Jessie. The unfortunate girl, it seemed, had grown a considerable beard when she was only in her teens, and for years nothing whatever had been done about it. "No man," declared Aunt Edith, "would have looked at her." Poor Jessie, it had been very hard for her. One day she had poured out all her feeling to David's aunt, who had been sympathetic but indignant.

"But, Jessie, why on earth don't you shave it off?" she had asked. "Nobody but you can do anything about it."

And Jessie had said, amazingly: "Daddy won't let me. He says God meant the hair to grow, and I must leave it be." And she had burst into tears.

But Aunt Edith cared nothing for fierce fathers and their beliefs. "Well, what about him? He shaves his beard off, doesn't he?"

There had been no answer to that one.

Poor girl! Throughout her childhood she had been terrified of her father, and I think she always had a deep respect for him. He was a strict Calvinist, and wielded a rod of iron over his family in the name of a wrathful God. Perhaps he honestly believed that God intended his daughter to bear her miserable disfiguration although she had the power to remove it; but it was possible – and there were murmurings in the town to this effect – that he wanted to keep her at home, proof against marriage, an invaluable slave. Be that as it may, some months after the talk with David's aunt Jessie went to Vancouver, and when she came back there was no beard. The tragedy was that by that time she was middle-aged, with greying hair and a set of cheap false teeth.

At times Jessie almost terrified me. That may sound unlikely, but it was true. Sometimes I could hardly bear to be with her, because she seemed like a kind of nightmare incarnation of my own old age.

She had straight, grey hair, scraped into a bun at the back, and cobweb-wispy around her face. She had frameless glasses, a flat chest, and queer, old-fashioned clothes. When she dressed up for town she put on an old-lady-ish, navy blue straw hat with white flowers, and in wet or windy weather she would tie over it a large, transparent plastic scarf.

"Shall I become like that?" I thought. "Hair in a bun, old dresses, when I can't afford hair-cuts or decent clothes? Glasses, cheap dentures and bony elbows when I am worn out with work? Pasty face, flat chest, thick stockings and a prickly chin, when I'm too happily absorbed in my own life to care about men? Oh, God forbid! I never prayed so fervently as when I was with Jessie. Jessie was the one who had said "Aren't we lucky? We have everything we want!" Jessie was the one who sketched trees and played her guitar, who wondered at the people who craved for their cities and movies when the simple life of the country had such riches to offer. And yet, while the rest of her family inspired me with admiration for their way of life, and with longing to imitate it, it was Jessie and Jessie alone who made me hesitate on the brink, even recoil from it in abject horror.

Sometimes I wanted to flee from her sexless presence and live in gorgeous wickedness with several lusty lovers! Often, out on the mountain with her under those lofty trees, or sitting beside her in the lake-lapped boat, I would long for even a minute's respite from her monotonous voice which told endlessly of people's operations and accidents, miscarriages and bereavements.

So morbid! She could make even her coyly smiling tales of young romance sound gloomy. But most of all I wanted to escape the shadow I saw in her of my future ugly, aging self, a shadow that grew darker and closer every time her mother unwittingly grouped us as contemporaries: "It's all very well for you young people," or, "Jessie's a grand girl," or, "So nice for Jess to have somebody else young about the place." Not "somebody young" but "somebody else young."

Oh, well, only a few years and I would be thirty, and that would make me feel so middle-aged that I might just as well be forty-five like Jessie. It seemed a shame to grudge her her illusion of lasting girlhood: I should want it myself when the time came. "Poor Jessie!" I thought. Yet I believed that she was, in her own way, happy.

CHAPTER TWENTY-FIVE

Buster used to set aside some of the full creamy milk for the house each day, filling as many pitchers as his mother put out; some he saved in the pails, to be diluted for the calves, and the rest he put through the separator. The petrol engine roared and chugged while he tipped the milk into the top of this astonishing machine; and, even before he had emptied the first bucket, two steady fountains sprang from the curved tubes at the bottom – one a thin twist of bluish-white milk, and the other a smooth arc of deep yellow cream. The skim-milk ran straight into the pig-bucket, and the cream into one of the heavy stoneware jars that the Harolds called cream-crocks.

I was amazed when I first realized that the cream was all sold to the Salmon Arm Creamery, nine

miles away. "But, Jessie, you only go over on Thursdays!" I exclaimed.

"Oh, in the summer we usually go to Canoe on Mondays too," said Jessie calmly. "We take it

over in the boat then, and ship it onto the train for Salmon Arm."

"But is it – is it all right?"

"How do you mean, all right?"

"Well, in this hot weather, with no frige or anything, doesn't it go off?"

"Oh, no, not in the cooler. Our cooler is as good as anybody's refrigerator. Isn't it, Buster?"

"Sure is," said Buster. "Every bit as good, if not a little better. But haven't you seen the cooler, Lavender? Jessie, I thought you'd shown it to her."

"And I thought you had!" laughed Jessie. She turned to me. "You must have a look at it in daylight some time. Buster made it, and we're very proud of it."

"Remind me after milking one day," said Buster, "and I'll show you."

But I forgot. Day after day I forgot – except, of course, at impossible times such as when I was out in the bush fetching the cows, or in bed. But a week or two later Buster did show me his pride and joy. It was another of his own good inventions, and did, indeed, do most efficient duty as a refrigerator. Housed in a bare, white room in the small building where the separator was kept, it consisted simply of two long wooden troughs, one over a foot deep and one about six inches deep, with water constantly running through. The water was icy cold, coming as it did straight from the creek, along the ditch in the woods and over the meadow in the high wooden flume. On a hot day it was heaven to stand under that flume in the leaky places, with the lush green grass and little bog-plants under one's bare feet, and the cold drips splashing on one's face and arms.

Once I saw a calf standing underneath with its tongue out, delicately catching and swallowing each drop as it fell. In the cooler, the tall cream-crocks stood in the deep trough, and the milk- jugs and jars of food in the shallow one; while around them the cold creek-water flowed slowly, to the left along one trough and back to the right along the other.

Although the cream kept well enough for making into butter, it could hardly have been retailed as fresh raw cream, for it often went a bit sour, especially in thunderstorms. I never knew it to turn rancid, but it did grow specks of downy mould, which Jessie used to skim off on the last morning just before it was taken to the boat.

On such mornings I would help her, fetching the full crocks one at a time from the cooler, and carrying them carefully across the yard and into the kitchen, where Jessie sat at the table "doing" them with a spoon. Slow and meticulous as ever, she peered critically at each one, skimmed off every particle of mould, and knocked off the half-spoonfuls of contaminated cream into a cat-dish. As she finished each crock Buster gave it a final inspection before emptying it into the big churn. "You can't be too careful," he said. "That's one thing we do like to do, sell clean cream. Never once since we've been selling to the Creamery have we had a complaint about dirty cream. I do think it is very important with food, don't you?"

I agreed emphatically.

"Now you'd be surprised," said Buster, warming up to his subject, "at some people. No idea at all. Flies in the cream every time, and all sorts. Do you know, I was talking to Jack, who works in the Creamery, and he said they had had to complain to one farmer. They'd always overlooked a few flies and the odd bit of mould, but this time they thought he'd gone a bit too far: when they emptied his churn they found a dead mouse in the bottom of it!"

There was never even a drowned fly in Buster's cream, for the cooler room had screens on the window, and a close-fitting screen door which everyone was very careful to keep closed; and there would certainly be no possibility of cream-sodden mice, unless some mouse learnt to swim running water and climb slippery, vertical jars.

The morning after my day in town, I had a wonderful time painting that cooler. The weather was dull but I was enjoying myself hugely. The previous day Buster had diverted the water, and emptied and cleaned the troughs; now I was painting the insides of them white. It took me all the morning, and I sang at the top of my voice the whole time, for the bare room had the flattering acoustics of a bathroom, and I was safely alone.

Buster and Jessie had gone to Salmon Arm in the boat and were away all day long. I fed and watered the horses at midday, finished thinning the sugar beets at last, and went cow-hunting on my own in the evening. I followed what must have been stale tracks up the logging road, and went right on past the path which I had taken the time I had met the bear. I felt very brave. The "road" vanished into a thicket of young cedars, but I pushed through until it widened out again, and went on further than I had yet been. I was quite a way beyond the top of the Canyon waterfall, close enough to the creek to hear it chattering softly over the stones, although it was hidden by trees, and although the roaring of the falls lower down still filled the air around me.

The falls thundered and hissed and rang, the creek tinkled and gurgled, and the dog beside me panted quickly, paused to swallow, and panted again. Through it all I strained my ears for the cow-bells, and heard their different notes everywhere, high ting, mellow dong, and deep clonk; yet there were no bells, but only the water.

It was very baffling and worrying. I went a few steps, listened again, went on once more.

Suddenly I forgot all my worries, because I came into a wide clearing where the creek ran broad and full over brown stones, and beside it were columbines growing wild. There were great tall clumps of them, with flowers as big as garden ones, each bloom a bunch of orange trumpets lined with yellow. The orange and yellow flamed against the vivid rain-washed greens of trees and grass, while overhead, in contrast, the sky hung grey and lifeless. Around the clearing stood the thick bushes and little trees, and overlooking them the tall trees; and behind the tall trees, unseen, unknown, the great mountain forests spread away for miles – whether uphill or down I could not tell. Nothing moved but the water, and I felt its eternal roaring and singing bearing down on me in the stillness, oppressive exactly as a great silence is oppressive. I began to feel uncomfortable and afraid, as if I were a trespasser here, and unseen eyes were watching me.

I pushed through the cedar thicket and went back down the logging road, with hardly a glance to either side, even at three shy mule deer that scudded away through the trees high above the trail. As I went down I let the fear grow on me, until I got the bear-horrors and saw a black bear in every burnt-out stump; and instead of searching further I went home, empty-handed and futile. But supper put fresh courage into me, and I took old Patch westwards once more, and this time found the cows at once. They were working their way homewards down near the shore, and were in one of the nearest clearings, and old orchard on a cliff-top over the lake, about a mile away from the farm. Jessie had told me of her own encounter with a bear there, but, illogically, because it was a long way from my bear place I was never afraid there.

As I picked my way home behind the leisurely line of little cows, I marvelled at the lake creeping steadily up the beaches, and wondered when its rising would come to an end. While it crept inch by inch here, in the vicinity of Salmon Arm it was rushing yard by yard. When I saw it yesterday it had reached up beyond the edge of the mud-flats and was beginning to invade the field with the Aberdeen Angus herd. I had found the whole landscape changed, and liked it better than before, for those mud-flats had been ugly. More than three quarters of the long wharf now stood over water, and the slipway at the end was almost submerged.

Over on our wild side of the lake, Buster often had to drag his little one-plank wharf a yard of two up the stones, and once he got the team to move the whole boat- house many yards up the beach. I drove them myself; and as I had to take them right up till they had their heads over the wire fence at the top of the beach, it seemed unlikely that the boathouse would be moved again that season whatever the lake did.

CHAPTER TWENTY-SIX

Because I love things made of wood I loved that big, strong, home-made cow-barn. Its walls and everything within them were wooden. The high, beamed roof was covered with hand-made shingles, grey with weathering; the stout rails between the stalls were the rounded poles of branches; and the floor was a platform of gigantic trunks, squared off and laid closely side by side. All of its timbers had been felled less than a hundred yards from the site, and still fulfilled one of the age-old functions of trees, that of sheltering animals; while the gap they left in the forest was used for growing good winter foods for cows and men.

Everywhere the congenial wood, unlike its modern substitutes, the impersonal steel and concrete, had adapted its character according to its use. The raised floor of each stall was gently hollowed by a thousand repeated pressures of little hoofs; the rails were smoothly rounded where the cow-chains were fixed to them; and there were areas of rich colour and high polish, edged with grease and stuck-on hairs, where the cows loved to rub their sides. Above, the old beams were dusky with spider webs and rough with the old droppings of swallows.

At milking times the herd wandered in from brilliant early morning sunshine or golden evening light, and small black hoofs pattered softly on the wooden floor as each cow went to her accustomed place. As long as nobody upset them, the cows never failed to go in their proper places; but once they were there, Buster and I used to chain them up quickly, or else they would change their minds and go out again. There was nothing in the mangers to tempt them to stay, for no cow was given her food until it was her turn for milking. Cows, like old people and children, love routine; they are not at all co-operative if things are done in a slightly different order from the usual. Buster's cows ate their cow-cake while they were being milked; one took the food to the stall along with the milk-pail and stool, and got busy as soon as the cow began to eat. If there was some delay and the cow finished eating before one began milking her, she would hold back at least half her milk, and there was very little one could do about it. It saved a great deal of trouble to learn the routine and stick to it.

An important part of Buster's milking routine was the initial cleaning of the udder, which he did entirely with his hands, never using water or cloth. He used to sit down on the stool with the milk-pail ready beside him, rest one hand on his knee, and with the other hand proceed to rub and stroke the udder and teats gently, firmly, until every particle of dirt had dropped off; often it was a full three minutes before he reached for the pail and began milking. The main idea was to avoid getting dirt and dust in the milk; but the cows obviously loved and benefited from the massaging. I learned to do it too, for it made a wonderful difference to the ease and speed of milking.

Knowing how particular Buster was about clean milk, I tried diligently, and sometimes successfully, to produce a pailful without a single speck of dust on the surface. One day I was milking a heifer - a great concession on Buster's part, and only the second time I had milked her – and both she and I were having a spot of bother over a mosquito, when suddenly, to my horror, she put a foot right in over the edge of the bucket. The bucket was more than half full, but by some miracle I got it away without spilling any milk; just one pale blob splashed up onto my jacket. The heifer's foot stamped back onto the floor, and she gazed round at me with bulging eyes and great frightened nose-blowing. I spoke to her and she soon calmed down, but I was very worried about the milk; I felt sure her foot had gone into it, and I did not like to milk any more into the same bucket with footy milk. I got up and stood holding the milking-stool and bucket, hesitating. Just then Buster came in.

"Oh, Buster, I've let an awful thing happen, I don't know what you'll say. She put her foot in the bucket. Yes. Oh dear, I'm most terribly sorry."

Buster came a little closer, and stood calmly behind the cow. All he said was: "I don't think she did Lavender."

This was staggering. "But she did," I insisted. "Right in. I know she did!"

But I could not convince him, and the cow's hind feet provided no evidence, because I had made some bad shots and squirted milk on both of them. Reluctantly I finished milking into the same pail; but when Buster put the milk through the strainer he said there was no trace of dirt in it. Either that foot had just missed the milk, or else it was an extra-ordinarily clean foot. As for me, I must have been born lucky.

I loved milking in that barn; and most especially I loved milking Annie. She was old and quiet and let down her milk easily; and from her stall one could see out through the alley way door the mountainside beyond the meadow, where soft green tree-tops rose steeply until they were out of sight above the doorway. No sky in this view – one could imagine that the trees climbed to infinity. At sundown golden beams would fall across in front of them, and sometimes, early in the morning, torn white rags of mist would be impaled up there on the pines. From the other stalls I had no such view, but I could always tell we were close under a mountain, for I could see a greenness through the high, dusty windows although there was no trees near the building.

Opposite to old Annie's place there were two horse stalls with high mangers and extra strong partitions. Buster usually brought Duke and Duchess in at the same time as the cows in the morning, and I liked to look at them while I milked, filling their outsize stalls and looking even taller and more powerful than usual. I liked to see their enormous, glossy rumps, and watch their lovely undocked tails switching at flies. Whenever a fly ventured too near, a shaggy hind foot would be raised, and there would be a tremendous and satisfying thud on the wooden floor.

When I was alone I used to listen to the milk in the pail, the munchings of cows and horses, the swishing of tails, or the grunting thump, followed by a huge sigh, of a cow lying down; but when Buster was milking with me I used to listen dreamily to his inexhaustible repertoire of stories. At first I had not been able to hear half of them, what with Buster milking into his pail across the way, and I into mine, the milk pinging onto the metal of the bucket right there between my ankles. Buster, at least twelve feet away, would hardly raise his voice above a whisper, and I would sit there trying to milk and listen at the same time. Sometimes I used to feel all angry inside because it was so difficult; I wished he would stop. Yet I hated to miss the entertainment, and in time I learnt to milk and hear both at once.

` "People sure do say the oddest things," said Buster on one of these occasions. "You know Cooke and that little yapping dog of his. He's crazy about it. Had it for nine years, and last winter when it got sick he was quite sick himself, worrying about it. Between you and me" - Buster lowered his voice even more that usual - "between you and me, if it had died nobody'd have been more pleased than me. Anyway, Jess and I were over there to tea one day last summer; I was logging over across the creek, Jess was helping me, and Mrs. Cooke asked us in to tea. While we were having tea Mr. Cooke dropped his teaspoon on the floor. It had a spot of tea on it, I guess, 'cos the dog went straight to it and licked it before he could pick it up. But he wouldn't let Jessie wash it or fetch him another. 'The dog's mouth is chemically pure,' he says. Chemically pure! I ask you!"

By the time milking was over most of the cows were usually lying down. Although Buster said they were nervous, they knew us and were not afraid of us, and we had a job to get them up. "This is how I do it, Lavender, look," said Buster, and he would step with the toe of his boot on the side of the cow's hoof, pressing down harder until the cow withdrew it sharply. Then he would tread on it again, or on another one, and the animal had to get up in self-defence. This method was neither hurtful nor frightening but it never failed to work. I often used it myself, and, although I trod only very gently on the small black cloven hoofs, my crepe-soled shoes were just as effective as Buster's heavy boots.

One little heifer – Daisy - was very sentimental and loved to have a particular spot on her throat rubbed; either Buster or I would give a minute or two rubbing that spot every morning and evening before unchaining her, without fail. Daisy's nose would tilt higher and higher, her eyes would half close, and she would grunt blissfully. It was gratifying to be able to give so much pleasure so easily.

I never untied the cows without first asking Buster, for sometimes he wanted one of them left in for some reason or another. Once he bought a young bull, and instead of putting him straight out in the corral he tied him up in old Annie's stall next to the alley way door, to keep him in for one night. Poor old Annie ad had to be shot the week before, rotten with mastitis. David was with us that day, and he had been watching Buster and me at the evening milking. While we were weighing the milk he began to unchain the cows, and soon Buster joined him, one of them working along each side of the gangway. David stopped at each stall and called across to Buster: "Shall I let her out?" And Buster answered: "Yes, David, please." When he got to the end stall David called: "This one okay? Shall I let her out?" "No, not her," said Buster. "She's the bull."

When we had been out late and milked after dark Buster lit two hurricane lamps and hung them on nails high on the stall partitions, and we worked in patches of warm, flickering light between lurking shadows. When Buster took milk to the separator-house he unhooked one of the lamps and took it on his arm; the darkness fled before him and leaped to close behind him, and he was nothing but a voice and a shadowy form beside his gleaming buckets and his swinging light.

We always worked quickly and silently at these times; we were usually very tired and anxious to get to bed. I loved the silence and the urgency, and the transformation of familiar objects in the lamplight. The barn felt safe and comfortable, but somehow mysterious; the cows were warm and sweet-smelling as ever, but their heads and bellies were hidden in shadows, and milking became a strange new magic.

CHAPTER TWENTY-SEVEN

Hot weather had begun again after a couple of dull days, and once more haymaking was in full swing. I spent the mornings turning hay with a fork, and the afternoons coiling it up. I had no hay-fever in the alfalfa, and much less than usual even in the ordinary hay, though whether this was due to the climate, the altitude, or my latest remedy I never knew. But even so, the cumulative effect of all this harvesting was, at the end of a day, like a 'flu coming on, combined with asthma, not to mention great physical tiredness. Sometimes it mad me very depressed.

On such occasions I was grateful to have the tonic of David, who teased me mercilessly. He used to turn up in the early mornings in his little row-boat, wearing a huge white topi, work hard for Buster all day, and have meals with us. At work he and I used to keep up an intermittent conversation which purported to be about Hong Kong and England, but which was actually a kind of flirtatious fencing-match. One day we were both turning hay, and he skimped his swath shockingly so as to catch up and work level with me. When he reached me he told me reproachfully the exact number of hours it had been since he had last seen me – forty-four and a half, I believe. At meals he would watch me and appear to be very shy, then break into a silence with a remark like "Say, can you cook, too?" Yes, David certainly kept up my morale.

Not that it always needed keeping up; I was finding farming infinitely more satisfying than typing or housework. I ate too much good farm food and was developing a tummy and a deplorable spare tire; I saw myself having to starve drastically in my next job. But I was very healthy and brown, and as tough as a horse. Recently I had been doing work for which I should not have had the strength a month earlier: one day I had removed two sledge-loads of wood from the saw-bench to the wood-shed, handling every great resin-oozing log twice; each one had seemed almost more than I could lift, yet I had gone on, fairly flinging them from the sledge onto the wood-pile, and had suffered no ill effect whatever. During dish washing I found myself picking up the full kettle from the back of the stove as if it were a small tea-cup, and remembered how I had once needed both hands to lift it, and had grunted with the effort.

On my fourth Sunday at the farm Buster and Jessie took me for the promised boat trip. They were still not satisfied: they wanted above all things to take me right to Mosquito Creek at the end of the lake; but that was thirty miles away, and we did not have time to go more than about twelve. We rounded the bend in the lake by Sicamous, but turned back when we reached Deep Gorge, a fierce some great cleft in the hills, full of great trees and deep shadow and the muffled roar of a creek. Buster was disappointed, and I had seen all I could want, for we had had a superb view up the lake, of the snowy Selkirks hanging in the sky, purple and white and delicately unreal.

We were out from mid-morning till 5:30 p.m. We cruised along fishing happily but in vain, and ate our sandwiches in the boat as we fished. I felt quite greedy because all my sandwiches were gone in a quarter of an hour, while Jessie's lasted her the best part of forty minutes. I failed to understand how anybody could eat so slowly.

After Deep Gorge we wound in our lines and got up speed, and on the way back found time to pay three social visits.

The longest visit was to the French Swiss people Jessie and I had seen on the ferry-boat the previous week. Their farm was on higher ground that the Harolds'. To reach it we landed in a little bay and climbed up steep steps between flowering shrubs; at the top there were the small fields, all hidden from the lake by trees. Mme. Perron and Mme. Paradis seemed overjoyed to see us: they were full of chatter and Gallic gesticulations. I found them a refreshing change from the Harolds, for they wore thin stockings and plenty of lipstick, and spoke of Paris intimately and enthusiastically.

Up at the house they introduced us to a mild old man whose relationship (if any) to themselves I never managed to figure out. He came from Switzerland and spoke only French, not a single word of English. Buster and Jessie knew no French, but they all seemed to get on excellently with signs and nods and much laughing. The old man got out his violin and played to us, then, eager to keep our attention, brought out more and more maps and picture postcards, to show us his native land. When I tried to talk with him in my poor, rusty, schoolgirl French he was so pleased that he almost wept. "Je vous montrerai," he said, running his shaky old finger excitedly over the feathery mountain shapes on the map. "Ah!" the finger stopped and pressed down intently on a particular spot. "Ici! Je demeurais ici, regardez. Vous comprenez?" I nodded vigorously. "Oui, oui, je comprends. Cettes montagnes, elles sont tres belles, n'est-ce pas?"

He beamed with pleasure and groped in a cupboard for more maps, more postcards. "Je dois vous les montrer, je dois vous les montrer... Ou...? Ah, les voici!"

While we talked French, I haltingly, he patiently, Buster's Western Canadian drawl mingled with Mme. Perron's broken English in a discussion of the prices of farm produce; odd phrases drifted across the room and cut incongruously into the Alpine vision and the French vocabulary: "Around four dollars seventy-five, I guess..." "She is onlee – how you say – a heifer..." All around us was a glorious French muddle. Pigs and poultry wandered where they pleased in the garden, the old man had a tear ten inches long in his shirt over on shoulder-blade, and there was a sick hen being nursed in a cardboard box under the sink.

Mme. Paradis insisted on giving us tea with delicious sandwiches and rich cakes, and I found her cooking even more delightfully French than her family's farming muddle. I was really sorry when at last we had to leave. Mme. Perron made me promise to come and see them again before I left. They all came to the foot of the steps with us, and the old man proudly showed us his new bateau, a smart little motor-boat with a cabin painted white and blue.

We were seen off with kisses and handshakes, waving and calling of last-minute good wishes; anyone might have thought we were going away for years.

As soon as we got back I went to fetch the cows. They were not far away, but because of the high water they had to swim twice on the way back, and milking was delayed until their coats had dried off. When chores were over at last it was well past ten o'clock; I was stiff and tired and glad to get to bed, but very happy.

CHAPTER TWENTY-EIGHT

Towards the end of June I decided to leave the Harold's on July 6th. Although I worked from early morning till late evening, sometimes up to 10:30 p.m., I still loved it there; but I wanted to go on to new places and gain fresh experiences, and I was longing for more young company. Perhaps, too, I was a little afraid that this job would become a habit with me, that I should never be able to free myself from the persuasive Harolds. But above all there was the urge in me, growing daily stronger, to continue my journey to the west. I must know what lay beyond Salmon Arm, I must see the Pacific. For no reason that I could have explained it was imperative that I should reach that other ocean; I could not rest until I had done so.

Meanwhile, with the end of my stay already in sight, I enjoyed this peaceful, backwoods life more and more. As I worked in the garden I looked up from time to time at the quiet hills towering over me, and the tall spiked trees climbing up them, and a great calmness came upon me. My "snow peaks," though they were becoming less snowy every day, looked as splendid as ever, especially when they glowed pink at sunset.

In the house, small domestic events took on a special significance. On June 27th we had the year's first strawberry shortcake for supper. Mrs. Harold's strawberry shortcake was a kind of local legend, and no wonder, for it was a dream of deliciousness, feather-light cake heaped with chopped strawberries and swimming in their fresh, sweet juice. Angel-food! We all had colossal helpings, I made a wish because it was the first time I had ever eaten this Canadian dish, and as for Buster, he took the big platter into the kitchen afterwards and licked it all over privately.

Buster Jessie licking platters after strawberry short cake
B's speciality
 N.B. these are not normal British Columbian manners!

Two days later, the last Thursday in June, Jessie had taken the ferry into town as usual; but this time her mother had gone with her to see the doctor. Mrs. Harold had had a bad knee for some time, having fallen downstairs on to it early that spring. It had been giving her a lot of pain lately – and no wonder, with all the work she did. At it all day, she was, from seven in the morning till ten or eleven at night, cleaning vegetables, washing dishes, standing over that volcano of a stove, and stopping to wash or scald an endless succession of milk pails and cooking pots on the kitchen floor. She sat down whenever she could, but that was not very often, and anyway she never let it stop her working. When she wasn't drudging in the kitchen she was drudging in the garden.

She would go out in the heat of the afternoon, and spend two hours or more bent into the most tiring of all postures, in order that the family might eat huge helpings of strawberries and cream for their supper. An old lady of seventy – nine! No wonder she was in pain.

It must have been severe pain that would make her leave her tyrannical chores for a day, go to the trouble of smartening herself up, and face the prospect of two boat trips and a dusty, footsore day in town. But suffering alone, however bad, would never have made her go; there had been plenty of persuasion by a worried family.

I had scant time for speculation about the doctor's verdict, for I found myself left in sole charge of three hungry men. David had turned up soon after breakfast, and, between showers, he and Buster were bringing in the hay we had coiled two days before. I spent a frantic morning producing enough cooked dinner for us all in the exact manner in which Mrs. Harold had instructed me to produce it, and at the same time cleaning the separator.

Although I seldom had to touch it the separator was already my pet aversion. It consisted of a dozen or so peculiar parts, every one of which had to be rinsed in cold water, washed carefully in warm, soapy water, and then thoroughly scalded. They were all awkward to wash, the most vital part being the worst. This last was a set of thirty-one nasty scratchy little metal plates with holes in them, which looked exactly alike but were numbered and had to be kept in their proper order by a gadget like a large safety pin, on to which they were threaded. They had to be taken off one by one, piled up in the correct order as they were washed, and then impaled on their pin again. A horrid, fiddly little job. By the time the whole separator was done my hands were soft and wrinkled with the soapy water. The one comforting thought was that it was Buster's job, not mine, to put the machine together when it was clean!

As long as the sun shone, Dr. Record sat on a chair in the garden and gazed between the apple- trees at the distant hay makers; but whenever there was a shower he came padding softly into the kitchen and watched me working. He told me one or two of his almost inaudible stories, and I missed all but a few sentences. Of all his soft- voiced family, the old man spoke the softest, and matters were not improved by the fact that he was quite toothless. He did have a set of false teeth, but refused ever to wear them, even for meals. Poor Mrs. Harold had to think up tempting foods that needed no chewing yet did not look invalidish; and his guests had to make good use of ears and imagination to enjoy his stories To judge by the confidential leaning forward, the positively wicked gleam in the old eyes, and the frequent use of the word "darned," these stories had more spice to them than Buster's. When he came to the end of one he would sit back and rock with a breathy, voiceless laughter so infectious as to do away with any need for appreciation of the joke.

When he was not telling stories he sat in the corner of the kitchen silently smoking his pipe, and I peeled potatoes self-consciously, afraid I was either too slow or not thorough enough. But the turquiose-blue eyes, brilliant under their bushy white brows, were not focused on me; the Doctor was far away among the shacks of pioneering Vancouver, in the dust-storms on the prairie, or in Kingston, where Canada's oldest university was but young when he was a student there.

I watched him, and thought what a remarkable old man he was. His white hair had not receded one smallest bit, and was as thick as a boy's. He was beginning to grow feeble, it was true – who does not at eighty? - and a close look at his eyes revealed a milky bar over the pupils and the greeny-blue irises; Mrs. Harold told me he could no longer read at all. But his hearing was far better than my own. So sensitive were his ears that he hated to have people around him who spoke less softly than his own family. If voices were raised in excitement, or in mistaken consideration for his age, he would get up and leave the room, or tap his glass for silence and demand quieter conversation in an awe-inspiring whisper. He had even been heard to complain bitterly of the noise the traffic made on the new road, spoiling the peace of his chosen countryside; though the said road was on the other side of the lake, more than a mile away. In learning to live in Dr. Harold's house I learned to live and think gently as well as to speak gently; and, growing to hate loud sounds myself, I acquired a new sympathy with cows and dogs and horses: though their ears are many times more sensitive than human ears, men will shout at them as if they were deaf. There was never any need to address the Harolds' animals in more than a normal speaking voice: usually a low murmur was understood and obeyed.

After lunch Dr. Harold went to have his rest, Buster and David returned to the urgent business of hay making, and I coped with the washing up alone. The showers were over, and outside the windows the lawn, hard and dry already, lay basking under a clear sky. I resented being in the kitchen. I hurried through the work, but it was after half past two when I finished. I hung up the last saucepan, put the knives away in the living-room (very quietly so as not to waken the old man in his bedroom behind the curtains), and went outside at last.

I washed my face, put on my sun-glasses, and set out across the meadow to get further orders from Buster. It was hotter than ever. The sun blazed down in the most soporific manner, grilling my shoulders, dampening the backs of my knees, and putting weights in my feet. I plodded on and on through the dry stubble, and as I plodded I marvelled at the way the house dwindled into the distance behind me while ahead the two men seemed as far away as ever. They were busy turning swathes with pitch-forks.

When at last I reached them David said: "Boy, I wish I could look nice in bluejeans!"

But Buster said: "Do you think you could manage the horse-rake?"

I hoped so! Nothing could have pleased me more. I raced back to fetch the horses from the stable, and found the distance no trouble at all. The rake was out in the meadow. Buster and David hitched the team to it, and I took the reins and climbed up into the high seat. Buster showed me the great lever which raised the tines to release the hay, and explained how I should work it with one foot so as to leave both hands free for the reins. It terrified me at first: I had to push it so hard I thought I should fall backwards off the seat, and when I did move it it clanked alarmingly, and my knee nearly knocked my chin in the process. But I soon got used to the idea, and before long there was a side strip of neatly combed stubble at one side of the field, marked at intervals with a roll of hay. Up and down, up and down I went, and the rolls grew out into long, thick lines across the field. I learnt to time the releases exactly right so that my lines came straight, and to leave the horses' mouths alone and let Duke do the steering: he knew far more about it than I did!

I was completely happy. The sun was on my back, and I had a handful of reins; two long tails switched the flies off two glossy rumps before me, and, beyond the rumps, four dear, stiff, responsive little ears listened to me, replied to me, and kept me constantly informed about their owners' feelings. All I had to do was drive up and down making this lovely simple pattern on the meadow; and at the edge of my growing work of art the mountains arose, lifting the forest to the very sky. Up in the canyon, out of sight, the crows cried hoarsely to each other. The tines rattled and rang behind me, and the horses' feet thudded on the thirsty land. I delighted in my growing skill, taking the machine within inches of the few apple-tree trunks, and ducking under the branches; and at the end of every row I rejoiced in the far greater skill of the horses – the way they turned in the minimum of spaces, the inner horse neatly crossing his feet, and the outer one walking round him.

When my straight rows were finished I raked along each one, driving Duke and Duchess right on the hay, and changed my striped design to a pattern of big dots, each dot a great pile of hay. I was amazed at the quantity of rakings that had come off what looked like a bare field. When it was done, Buster left his swath-turning, changed the horses to the wagon, and brought in two or three good loads from the results of my afternoon's work.

"Boy! said David as I climbed down from my iron perch, "Can all English girls drive horse- rakes?"

Tired but satisfied, I walked back to the house. Five o'clock: I must have been raking for over two hours, no wonder my seat ached! But there were more jobs yet to be done: laying the table, then fetching the cows.

The cows had gone east and were not far off; but they had chosen a clearing that I had not seen before, high up on the steep mountainside where wild syringa bushes fairly sang with the joy of their white blossoms, and the bees gave voice to their song. The air was filled with the sweet heady scent, and everywhere in the grass fat, red strawberries hung on delicately curved stems. I sat down and gazed and sniffed and ate, ate and sniffed and gazed, and tried to understand such profusion of beauty but found it beyond me.

Cows the colour of sunlit sand moved, dark-eyed, between the white bushes, and their bells rang beautifully against the low plainsong of the bees. Down below me were bold pagodas of cedar and feathered traceries of hemlock, and below them again, behind and beyond them, lay the widespread calm of the shining lake, perfect in its scalloped frame of dark headlands.

If it had not been for Patch I might have sat on for hours in the June sunshine, tasting and smelling, touching, hearing and watching the wild loveliness of the world. But the old dog's idea of bliss was connected with a certain dish under the kitchen table, and he was anxious to get home. For once he started rounding up the cows on his own. Deep-throated barks and frantic bell-ringing roused me, and I went to help Patch, for the cows hated going downhill and were being difficult. With a little cooperation we got them going, and soon we were winding our way in and out along the lake shore. I pulled my watch out of my pocket (I never wore it on my wrist during the day, the bright metal strap seemed to attract all the flies and mosquitoes): it was nearly six-thirty. Ten minutes later, as I came scrambling over the rocks on Larch Point, the ferry boat was just backing away from the Harolds' little wharf, and Buster and Jessie were helping one very tired old lady up the beach.

When I got in, everyone was in the kitchen, Mrs. Harold sitting on her hard washing-up stool in the corner. "It's not going to be that easy, Buzz," she was saying, "but I guess if he says to rest I will jest have to rest." She turned to me. "The doctor says I must rest an hour in the morning and an hour in the afternoon, every day," she explained. "I'm afraid we'll have to ask you to help Jessie in the house a bit now, it's going to be a lot of work for her. I know you'd rather be outside, and I know Buster needs you too, but -"

"Of course I'll help," I said. "That's what I'm here for. I'm just so glad you really are going to rest, and look after yourself for once."

"There, you see, Mother?" said Buster. "Everybody says the same."

"It's what we've all been telling her for three months or more," said Jessie, "but it takes a visit to the doctor to make her do it."

"Not a bit of use me being a doctor," murmured Dr. Harold, and laughed squeakily.

"And we're all going to see that you keep it up, Mother," said Jessie, ignoring him.

"I think you ought to make a start right now," said Dr. Harold. "You come and sit somewhere softer than that durned old stool, and let Jessie and Lavender get the tea. Come on, Mother."

Buster helped his mother into the living-room, and the old man followed with his stick. "What a pathetic couple they are," I thought with a sudden wave of affection for them, "and how uncomplaining."

As the table was already laid we had only to bring in salad and cheese, bread and jam and fruit. In a few minutes Jessie said: "There's only the tea to make, now, Lavender. You run over to your cabin and read your mail. You're a lucky girl this week, four letters; I put them on your table." The week's mail! Why, I had forgotten all about it. Three of the letters were from home, and one from Den.

Whether it happened that evening or very early next morning I could never remember, but within twenty-four hours of Mrs. Harold's return I found myself committed to stay over at the farm an extra week: I should be leaving on the 13th of July now, instead of the 6th. I foresaw a lot of gloomy housework in those two remaining weeks, and quailed at the thought; but after all, how could I begrudge these people one more week of my time? I was free, Den had not yet found me a job in Vancouver, and the Harolds needed the help so very much. Tired as I was, I seemed to see those fourteen days stretching before me into the dim future, fourteen days of sweated labour, of ignominious housework. But if I pulled myself together and thought of the thing sensibly I knew two weeks was nothing, and that when it came to an end I should be sorry to leave. In two weeks Mrs. Harold might have recovered completely, and then I would feel I had achieved something by staying.

I made the condition that I should have one more full day off, staying over in Salmon Arm for a nigh t as before; and the thing was fixed.

CHAPTER TWENTY-NINE

I had been right about the gloomy housework. For Mrs. Harold's two hours of resting it seemed that I had to do four hours of extra housework every day. Though I tried to look cheerful and willing I did not always feel cheerful inside. I could let off steam only in the privacy of my cabin, and that Friday I confided sadly to my diary that I had worked in the house all morning. "A beastly washing up," I wrote, "including the separator. Most depressing, in spite of a nice swim before lunch. Almost weepy by afternoon."

I spent two hours of that afternoon picking strawberries, wearing my sun-bra and Jessie's old straw hat. Though it was more pleasant to have sun on my back than steam in my face, I sympathized afresh with Mrs. Harold whose job this usually was. For a while I would work crouching right down; then when my ankles ached too much, and the sweat literally ran from the backs of my knees, I would straighten my legs and hang over the plants with my seat in the air and the blood running to my head. Mrs. Harold invariably worked in the latter position, though with slightly bent knees: no wonder she was permanently doubled over.

Never let it be thought that strawberry-picking for the Harolds was a simple matter of getting all the red ones and leaving the rest: even though we usually ate them all ourselves, nothing but perfection would do; one must never pick a strawberry unless it was exactly the right shade of red. This meant that every fruit on every one of those prolific plants must be gently lifted and critically judged, and often luscious-looking ones must be left for another day because they were not quite up to the Harold standard.

I helped at several pickings before I learnt just what was required, having to ask again and again, like a small child, "Is this one all right?" Often I was amazed when Mrs. Harold inspected what I thought was a good ripe one (with perhaps a minute patch of white on it) and said: "No, Lavender, we never pick them green." Sometimes she went over my basket afterwards and even criticized the ones I had been quite sure about, sure enough to pick without asking.

Mrs. Birmingham, David's mother, was not far wrong when she said the Harolds all but took the temperature of each strawberry and raspberry before they picked it.

That afternoon I was as glad to leave the strawberry bed as I had been to leave the kitchen in the morning. But every hardship has its compensations: that was the day that I lay in the Larch Point pasture and watched the mother gopher with her five babies.

That was the day, too, that I did the milking alone so that Buster and David could bring in late loads of hay. I had a delicious sense of personal responsibility, almost of ownership, as I brought the herd in, chained and fed them, and reaped a threefold harvest of yellow, frothing milk. I loved the cow-barn more than ever: the dusky warmth, the deep animal content of the place, soaked into my very being; and the muscular rhythm of milking soothed my mind and body almost as though it were the fulfillment of an instinct. Sometimes I am inclined to think that milking cows has become a human female instinct: why not, when it has been the right and proper work of woman for countless ages? It affords the wholly feminine satisfaction of divine creation through simple physical effort. Butter-making has the same quality: an intense pleasure comes from the exhausting, unskilled labour and the simultaneous miracle of smooth cream changing to rough granules under one's very hands.

The following day, Saturday, was July 1st and a Canadian holiday; but the Harolds observed no holidays except Sundays either for themselves or their helpers. I was in the kitchen all morning washing, drying, and putting away dishes, peeling potatoes, and dealing with those everlasting strawberries. I almost began to hate the sight of strawberries. Every single one I had picked in those two hours the previous day had to be shucked, cut in half, and put on the "platters" ready for tomorrow's strawberry shortcake. Even the smallest blemish must be removed with the knife. It was a long job, but the results looked good – three huge dishes quite full of bisected berries, three jumbled heaps of seed-stippled red and smooth, flat white. Mrs. Harold came and helped me for the final ten minutes. When it was all done she covered the fruit generously with sugar shovelled out of a hundred-pound bag, put them under meat- covers in the alley-way, and left them to ooze out their syrupy juice all the afternoon.

Saturday dinner was always the big meal of the week: roast beef, roast potatoes, vegetables and gravy, apple pie and tea. Everyone had gigantic helpings of everything, especially apple pie: Mrs. Harold made two full sized Canadian-style pies with crust underneath as well as on top, and the five of us nearly always finished the lot. Buster had two helpings, each consisting of a quarter of a pie, no less. It had been one of his ambitions as a boy to eat a whole pie, and he had achieved it – but only once.

The crockery to be washed up seemed to fill the kitchen, and most of it was dreadfully greasy. I coped with it alone, and it took me well over an hour, during which time two pairs of gay, holiday-mood visitors turned up. Twice the living-room door opened to receive them, and twice it shut on an increasing hum of conversation. As a rule I dislike social chit-chat, but now I felt as people-starved as the Harolds themselves, and wished I could get clear of the kitchen and join in the fun. I finished the plates and glasses and knives and forks, but the crowd of cooking-pots on the floor seemed only to multiply as I worked my way through it. After a while the living-room door opened and the visitors were escorted out through the alley-way into the garden, and taken off to do the round of the buildings. Nobody looked into the kitchen. I had waves of self-pity, and a growing sympathy with Shakespeare's Greasy Joan keeling her wretched pot.

Then Buster appeared suddenly and quietly at the window. He put his head in and looked sympathetic. "Well! Poor little Lavender! Still washing dishes, eh? Never mind, they'll soon be done now." He inclined his head in the direction of the buildings. "You're not missing much," he said confidingly. "Dave and I got away just in time, to the hay. We've just finished carrying the little piece this side of the berry patch; we could do with you to rake it, too." He helped himself to a dipper full of water from the tub inside the window and drank it slowly. "You bring the team out," he said, reaching in to hang the dipper on its nail, "as soon as you've finished in here, okay? Dave and I will be somewhere about, and the rake is where you left it on Thursday. Okay?"

I nodded, much cheered. "Okay."

I raked for an hour. I was too tired to make a good job of it, but fortunately nobody seemed to mind. Then I fetched the cows; they were a long way off and I came back more tired than ever. Supper was so late that we were milking after dark, but I was more cheerful by then. The food had put new life into me, and round the supper-table the Harolds had been full of laughter and infectious high spirits. Their rare social contacts always did them good, and were always greatly appreciated; though the Harolds never considered these influxes of "company" to be rare at all.

"People will keep asking us if we don't get lonely out here," said the Doctor. "Lonely! There's always people dropping in." He leaned towards me confidentially and lowered his voice. "But if you ask me, they don't come to see us. They all get to know about Mother's strawberry shortcake: if they haven't tried it they drop in on the off chance, and once they have had it they keep coming back every year for more. Hee! Hee! Hee!" I laughed with him and he immediately became serious. "It's true!" he said earnestly. I believed him about the shortcake, but I knew that that was not the only thing people came for. Whether they were old friends or just curious trippers, all who came up the lake wanted to see the Harolds themselves. And nobody was disappointed; the Harolds were always very much themselves, and visitors were invariably given strawberry shortcake if it was mid-summer, and friendliness and hospitality at any time of the year.

CHAPTER THIRTY

My break came next day – and just in time, before the work piled up on me too much. Buster was generous and gave me Sunday afternoon as well as the whole of Monday. I had had an invitation from David the night before, to come over to his mother's for Sunday tea, and that fitted in nicely with the plans of the Harolds: they were having friends to lunch, and the friends in turn were to take them out all afternoon.

Although it was Sunday, milking was at the usual time, and once again I drudged in the kitchen all the morning; but after that things brightened up. Soon after twelve there was a scuffle behind the cow-barn, and all three dogs went tearing down over the meadow, tails waving and hackles up. The noise was deafening: deep-throated barks from Patch, ridiculous echoes from the self- important Blackie, and Tess's nervous, high- pitched yaps continuing long after the others had stopped. They all ranged up and down the fence until Jessie went down and let them through onto the beach, and at that moment the guests appeared round the point in a small boat with an outboard motor. Jessie brought them up to the house, there was much handshaking all round and I, as usual, was introduced as "Miss Longstaff, our farmerette."

Lunch was a lively affair which included the famous strawberry shortcake and several of Buster's best stories. I liked the visitors: Mr. Vernon was an Englishman with a pointed black beard, and his wife was Swedish and very attractive. They were full of enthusiasm for their lake shore farm which they had bought only a few months ago. And were longing to show it to the Harolds. They were full of questions for Buster: Mr. Vernon was familiar with agriculture, but only in England; and his wife, bravely facing the responsibility of a future dairy herd in spite of a complete lack of experience, was anxious to learn all she could. Buster answered their questions with his usual gentle assurance; after lunch he took them both on a tour of the cow barn and separator-house. Mrs. Harold, who seemed to be dispensing with her two rests that day, did the washing up herself and Jessie helped me to dry. Everything was finished by two o'clock, and we all went down to the boathouse.

Dr. H., Mrs. H., self, Jessie, Norman, Buster.

Leaving Birmingham's after tea.

Buster and Jessie together pushed the boat down the rollers into the water, Buster brought it round to the wharf, and Jessie filled it with rugs and cushions, and helped her parents in. Meanwhile the Vernons had untied their own small boat, climbed in and started up.

I stood on the shingle, watching and waving while the two craft swung out in a curve round the point, the Vernons leading the way to their farm and the Harolds following suit; then I ran back to my cabin and changed. My clothes hung in a kind of wardrobe I had improvised by pushing the hooks of several coat-hangers through a hole in a large sheet of newspaper and hanging them all together on a six-inch nail on one of the highest beams in my roof. The result was an unsightly bundle, but I had to protect my dresses from dust somehow, and did not want to leave them squashed in my suitcase. Other nails in the roof accommodated such things as a mirror, sponge-bag and brush- and-comb-bag. I reached up under the newspaper now, and slipped a green and white dress off its hanger. I had not worn a dress for a week: I felt like a chrysalid changing into a butterfly. The jeans and T-shirt, which had acquired the monotony of a uniform, I folded and put away under the bedspread with a grunt of satisfaction. I exchanged the clumsy brown shoes for a pair of white ones, used lipstick for the first time in ten days, and felt deliciously feminine.

As packing consisted merely of putting wash-things, nightdress and hand-bag into a paper carrier, I was ready early. David had promised to collect me "after lunch" in his boat, but I did not expect him much before three o'clock. So I sat in my cabin and admired the flowers, particularly the day-lilies. Today two frail bronze-coloured blossoms showed among the row of pale green clumps outside my door. The lilies had only begun to flower a few days ago, and I loved them for their transient beauty: though they shrivelled and died after one brief day there were always two or three fresh blooms to take their place next morning. Four or five brilliant blue delphiniums grew below the window behind me, and just out of sight was the lilac bush, which propped its branches comfortably all over one corner of my roof. I could hear humming birds zooming and whistling among its few late blooms, and the sweet scent pervaded the hut.

The lilies of the valley were over now, but their broad, pointed leaves still spread half way round my little house. All through June crowds of creamy white flowers had hidden beneath them, whose scent had so engulfed the cabin that I could have found my way there blindfolded. Jessie had sold and given away dozens of bunches, and I had always kept a vase full on my table. Now the vase held a gay bunch of Indian Paintbrush which I had picked in the woods – a more appropriate decoration for a log cabin on the edge of the bush.

For an hour there was no sign of David. At first I lay on the lawn and gazed up at the deep blue sky; I relaxed every muscle and rejoiced in my solitude and idleness. Then I began to make repeated excursions to the gate on the hopes of seeing the familiar blue boat nosing round the point, with the oarsman in his white topi. Finally I got into the little old dinghy and pushed off into the bay. I don't know what prompted me: perhaps a wish to show off my rowing to David, just restlessness. After I had rowed a few yards it crossed my mind that I might take the dinghy the whole two miles and save David a journey – Buster had said I could use it as much as I pleased. But then I remembered that there would be nobody to bring it back from the Birmingham's, and that I would miss David if he happened to be walking over instead of rowing. I rowed around in a circle, and decided to wait, but just then there was a splash and a shout behind me:

"Hi," said David.

We landed side by side and pulled our boats up onto the beach. David surveyed my clothes approvingly. "So you're a girl after all!" he said.

He took my paper carrier and raincoat and put them in the bows of his boat. "Is this all you're taking?"

"Yes."

"Have you got your swim-suit in here?"

"No."

"You'd better fetch it, you and I are going to go swimming."

I fetched it, and an hour later David and I were swimming lazily in the shallow waters by Birmingham's cabin. The lake was really warm here, and for the first time I believed what Jessie had said about there being cold springs under Harolds' bay: I had never considered it specially cold, and until now had expected the whole lake to be the same. Harolds' bay was not an ideal bathing place: the shore level dropped too steeply, and the surface there was smeared with great patches of pale yellow pollen which drifted out from under the poplar trees on the beach and stuck all over one's body as one came up out of the water. Jessie told me many people were allergic to it, and came out in rashes after bathing; fortunately it did not affect me in that way.

But here at Birminghams' there were no trees near enough to the lake to shed their pollen on the water, and down under the clear ripples our moving limbs looked like polished brass. It was a great luxury to swim just for the fun of it. Every day for three weeks I had been bathing only for the sake of cleanliness and refreshment, and always in a feverish rush just before dinner. Today I had David to talk to, and, it seemed, all the time in the world. When we had swum enough we lay on the wooden wharf and let the broiling sun dry us; and when we were dry David's mother called us in for tea.

Tea! Proper, English, afternoon tea, with bread and butter, jam and cakes, and the certain knowledge that there would be another meal between it and next day's breakfast! We had it on the verandah of the wooden cabin with the wall of Mrs. Birmingham's bedroom behind us, and on the other three sides of us nothing but mosquito screening, with the lake twinkling and rippling beyond it. Across the water the white houses of Canoe clustered under the green bench lands like butterflies' eggs under a leaf; and above and beyond them, prouder and lovelier than ever in russet and purple, the twin peaks of Mount Ida dominated the scene.

Mrs. Herald, Mrs. Birmingham (Jennie), Jessie

In the midst of all this wild loveliness our teacups chinked on our saucers less and less often, as the conversation passed from farming and fishing to the latest books, and from the latest books to religion and philosophy. Suddenly I remembered having tea in the lounge on the ship five months ago, and the English doctor telling me about British Coumbia. "A farmer can work all day with you and then sit down under a haystack and talk philosophy. Do you see what I mean?" How right he had been, and how well, how well I saw his meaning.

Later that evening I felt more than ever well-disposed towards British Columbians. David had arranged a lift for me with a middle-aged couple nearby who owned a motor launch and were returning to town after a weekend at their summer cabin; these kind people had rushed me at exhilarating speed to Salmon Arm, had refused to take any kind of payment, and had extended the good turn to include a lift in their car from the wharf to the hotel.

At the hotel I checked in, rang Mrs. Meek, and checked out again immediately: Mrs. Meek had asked me to stay the night, and was coming right away to fetch me in her car!

That was the night I saw my second bear. Mrs. Meek had put me in the "Monkey-house," a dear, funny, little room, hardly more than a verandah, which opened out of her own bedroom. It was built in an angle of the house, and two of its walls were the untouched boards of the outer house-walls, rough and weathered; its other two sides were open except for mosquito screening and a three-foot high boarding round the base. The floor was a wooden platform built only a foot from the sloping ground at one end and supported on five-foot posts at the other. I had seen the Monkey-house from the outside and knew that in the sheltered corner underneath it long grass grew, and dead leaves were scattered, and a wild blackberry vine trailed to meet the straggling branches of some garden shrub. It was on the side of the house where the lawn became lost under pine needles and cones, where venturesome butterflies hesitated and turned back into the sunshine, where the garden merged into the bush.

Sleeping in the Monkey-house was like sleeping out, but without the insects or the risk of rain. Tall spruces stood just outside, and from my narrow camp bed I could see their straight trunks standing black against the night sky:

they had rough, knobby bark, and were whiskered with a few dead twigs, long and curved and brittle. Up higher, the night air moved almost imperceptibly through their branches, touching the low chords of pine-needle music so gently that I was deeply stirred without knowing the reason why. Dead needles fell whispering onto the roof, and sometimes a mouse would rustle through the dry leaves down below the floor.

I switched on the lamp and read awhile, and golden moths whirred and banged against the rusty screen. When I switched it off, the screen became invisible and the moths were but dark specks drifting away into the night. I snuggled into the comforts of re-living an idle day and anticipating a late rising and an idle morrow; and soon my ordered gloating was lost in a vague flow of dreams.

Suddenly I was jerked back to consciousness by a terrific noise outside, a blundering and bustling and twig-snapping, shattering the silence of the night. It seemed to come from away up behind the house, and grew louder and louder every moment: something was coming down the mountainside as if its life depended on it – something big. I sat up, tensed and ready to leap out of bed if the thing should come near enough for me to see it. Perhaps it was an escaped horse? Perhaps a mule deer – two, three, four mule deer – pursued by a cougar! Perhaps... In a few seconds there flashed through my mind countless visions of the various wild things that it might be, and their possible motives for crashing so noisily through the darkness. I put a foot out on to the floor and craned my neck, but could see nothing. The noise grew so loud that I half expected to see a couple of mad carthorses gallop right into the garden; there was a split-second pause, a violent scrabbling, then dead silence; and there, plumb in the middle of my view and not ten paces away, was a half-grown bear cub.

He had stopped a few feet up one of the nearest trees and was hugging the trunk like a Koala bear. I could not tell whether he was looking at me or away from me, but I could see the teddy-bear shape of his head with its fuzzy round ears silhouetted against the night sky above his black teddy-bear body. There he stayed, quite still, excited, alertly watching, getting his breath back. Such a little fellow to have made so much commotion! I did not believe he had been chasing anything, or that anything had been chasing him: it had just felt grand to be a young cub running downhill faster and faster, and so he had run. And when one has run downhill that fast, what could be more fun than to let the impetus carry one halfway up another hill, or better still, up a tree? That was just what he had done, and now there he was, half exultant, half afraid, surveying the world from the grand height of ten feet up a spruce tree.

For a long moment both he and I remained motionless. I called softly to Mrs. Meek to come and look, but she must have been asleep. At last the cub slithered noisily down to the ground, and a minute later I heard him shambling around in the dead leaves underneath my floor grunting and blowing. Then he padded quietly off, and though I jumped out of bed and peered into the darkness outside I did not see him again.

In the morning I was woken early by the squirrels screaming at each other in the trees and, apparently, practising tap-dancing among the spruce needles on my roof: there seemed to be even more wild life here than at the Harolds'. The Meeks showed interest but not surprise when I told them about the bear cub, though Mr. Meek doubted whether it would have climbed more than a yard up the tree. I took him outside before breakfast, and together we found the fresh, red scratch-marks in the bark, reaching to ten feet up. But we could not find a sign of a track anywhere, there had been too many squirrels about.

CHAPTER THIRTY-ONE

When Mrs. Meek drove down to Salmon Arm to work I went with her, and we took her bicycle, strapped onto the back of the car, for me to return on. I did some shopping, and at her "office" she gave me another badly-needed shampoo and set. I tried hard to pay her for it, but she refused as before. "Don't be so silly," she said, quite angrily. "I wouldn't hear of it: I should be very hurt if you paid me. NO, no, I mean it. Go on, put it away, now." I eventually put the money back in my purse, and she looked happier at once. "It is horrible being in business," she said.

"I loathe and detest asking people for money, telling them how much to pay each time I do a job. It's bad enough taking payment from ordinary customers, but one has to. But when I do a friend's hair, like yours, and do it as a friend, well.... Let's forget all about it now, anyway. Sometimes I wondered how she had ever made any money at all. And to think that one person in Toronto had told me the British Columbians were "so crude!"

I left her after lunch and toiled back up the long hill in the blazing sunshine. I had to push the bicycle more than half the way, and I went slowly, leaning my arms and chest on the handle-bars and letting my toes skid in the gravel at the side of the road. At the top of the hill I turned into the lanes to escape the traffic, and joggled idly along, zigzagging to avoid the worst of the bumps. The grass on either side was white with dust, and under the clear blue sky everything was drenched in heat and light. Three blue butterflies danced across the stones, and high in the hedge the wild roses were deeper pink than ever. I saw a Red Admiral fluttering over some thistles, and a little further on a Comma was basking on a leaf. I began to count butterflies, and took so long getting back to the house that Mrs. Meek, her work over, arrived there before me.

Canoe B.C.

After tea I walked down to the cross roads and caught the "bus" to Canoe. I was the only passenger this time, but in Canoe a long queue was waiting to go back to Salmon Arm, and there at the end of it, bearded and grinning with his thumbs tucked into his braces, was Buster. "It sure is good to see you again," he said. He took my feather-weight luggage gallantly and escorted me to the wharf as if I were a great lady.

Dr. Harold was waiting in the boat in place of Jessie; he was a great deal less talkative than his daughter. Just a lift of his hat, a twinkle in the old eyes, and a "Back to the grindstone now, Lavender;" then Buster started up the outboard motor and we all three sat in silence, peacefully following our own separate thoughts. The only sound was the steady put-put-put of the motor, and even that lay on the hushed evening air as becomingly as our curving wake lay on the silken water. Once Buster shut it off, and we drifted in a sudden overpowering quiet. "Cows have gone west," he said softly. "Anybody hear them?"

Small ripples jostled past the sides of the boat, and across the water I could just hear a low, steady hiss which must have come from the Canyon falls; but there was no other sound. So beautiful was the reflected light that it seemed to me we were floating on a fallen fragment of the sky, caught and held between the watching mountains. I forgot to go on listening.

"There!" said Buster. He put his head on one side and closed his eyes for a moment. "Yes, over there." He pointed in the direction of the Birminghams' cabin.

"I can't hear anything," I said.

"I can. Somewhere by Birminghams'. Listen."

We all listened again, and this time the old man said he, too, could hear the bells; but I could not hear a thing.

"You go along past Birminghams' tonight, and I think you'll find them okay," said Buster, and he started the motor again. When we landed I collected the dogs and walked that way, and, sure enough, there were the cows, just where Buster had said.

I had gained new strength from my holiday. Next morning, for the first time in weeks, I woke up easily and was dressed long before Jessie came to call me. Instead of dragging myself unwillingly from under a great weight of sleep, I was able to leave the world of dreams in an instant, opening my eyes into a glory of sunshine, lake and trees, and feeling at once the happy urgency of the work to be done.

But this pleasant state of affairs did not last many mornings, for work was hard that week. Dr. Harold was unwell and Mrs. Harold herself not fit to do more than look after him. Harvesting was still not finished, and although David came every day, often turning up before breakfast and always working till after dark, labour was short. Jessie and I worked in the house a great deal of the time, and I had to spend long hours picking strawberries in place of Mrs. Harold. When we could, we helped in the hay, Jessie doing noble work with a pitch-fork and hand-rake, and myself driving the horse-rake whenever possible, in the hopes of avoiding hay-fever. And all the time the weather grew hotter and hotter.

In the garden, weeds grew apace: hay-making was top priority now. Buster was anxious to get all his harvesting done before the weather broke, or before the hay spoiled in the heat. Most of it was alfalfa, and if alfalfa is allowed to dry out too much its leaves drop off, rendering it almost useless.

One stifling afternoon, when the hay was nearly all in, a thunderstorm broke over us, and the vertical rods of rain beat down with incredible fury, on and on, drumming with sickening monotony on the ground and on the roof. The sky was an angry yellow colour, and indoors it was quite dark except during the lightening flashes. The thunder rolled about among the mountains like a sulky giant muttering to himself, with no pause between the last echo and the next new crash. Buster and David, who had been watching the sky and working at top speed, came in with their clothes clinging to them and their dripping hair plastered to their foreheads, and stood about in the alley-way avoiding the worst drips from the leaking roof.

"We just weren't quite quick enough," said Buster.

"How much have you left out, Buzz?" asked Mrs. Harold.

"Two," said Buster. "Two loads, maybe three little ones."

Everybody made sympathetic noises.

"We did our best," said David.

"Dave's been working like three men," said Buster. "I can't grumble."

"I'm sure you've both worked harder than anybody ever should do," said Mrs. Harold. "It's jest a pity the rain couldn't have held off one more day."

"We can't have everything," said Dr. Harold.

But the next day was hotter than ever, and the hay was dry enough by midday for loading. That afternoon everyone turned out to watch the last load going up into the barn: the harvest was over at last.

The sun blazed down mercilessly. The rain had hardly penetrated two inches into the rock-like earth, and the greasy surface turned back into dust in a few hours. The cabbages I had planted out in the wet earth the evening before were poor little flopped things, limp and grey, and I felt just as floppy myself. Once, when I had five minutes to myself between jobs, I found the ideal way of using spare time. I lay flat on my back on the lawn with my arms and legs spread out like a star-fish, and relaxed every muscle in my body: I swear I could feel the tiredness draining out of my very toes and finger-tips.

That evening Mrs. Harold went to bed with a chill, and Jessie and I cooked the supper. I did the long washing up alone, milked late, and washed all the milk things for Buster, which took me until after eleven o'clock. I reckoned I had worked fifteen hours during the day.

It was on that same day that my successor was appointed. Just before lunch there was uproar among the dogs, and Buster went down to the beach to meet an unexpected visitor who was pulling a small, battered dinghy up onto the shingle. They came up the path together, Buster looking slim and positively graceful beside his new companion, who was taller than himself but immensely, flabbily fat.

"This is Norman Lundy, said Buster. "My father, Dr. Harold; Mother; my sister Jessie; Miss Longstaff."

Norman held out a chubby red paw and gave each of us a codfish handshake.

"This may be just the person we're looking for," said Buster. "He's looking for a job. Isn't that right, Norman?"

"Yeah," said Norman. "They told me you had a job for me here, so I thought I'd come and find out."

The Doctor raised his eyebrows and opened his mouth to speak, but his wife laid a restraining hand on his arm. "We were just going to have our meal, Norman," she said. "Will you come and have it with us?"

"Sure," said Norman, and we all went in. The old man muttered something under his breath, but nobody paid any attention.

Norman was young and fair-haired, with a round, surly face, high colouring, and a crew cut. The bridge of his nose was broad and puffy, and his mouth hung open: these things gave him a moronic look, but as soon as he spoke one realized they were caused only by adenoids.

Jessie laid an extra place for him between Dr. Harold and myself, and we all tried not to notice his manners, which were appalling. He sat hunched over his plate with both elbows stuck out, shovelled his food into his mouth and chewed it noisily. When his plate was empty he wiped the back of his hand across his face.

"Do you wish any more, Norman?" asked Mrs. Harold.

"Uh?'

"I said, do you wish any more?"

"Oh, yeah." He put his knife and fork on the table and handed me his plate,

which I passed to Mrs. Harold; when I gave it back he took it with both hands and delved straight into it: never a word of thanks. Mrs. Harold rolled her eyes at me; I didn't dare look at Buster. I concentrated instead on the white flowers on the damask tablecloth; and once, when I glanced across at Jessie, I saw that she too was taking an unusual interest in the design.

Norman did not speak much during the meal, but when he did his voice was loud and coarse. It would have been loud enough anywhere, but here, in contrast to the gentle murmurings of the Harolds, it was earsplitting. Dr. Harold retreated into an angry silence, quivering with the effort of self-control. After lunch Buster took the boy out to show him the farm and discuss the work; and as soon as they had gone the old man's eyes blazed.

"If Buster takes on that great lump," he said, "I won't have him eating in my house."

"What else could we do? We couldn't make him eat alone in the kitchen, it wouldn't seem right," said Mrs. Harold. "Besides," she added, "it would be so awkward."

"He should take his meals with the dogs," Dr. Harold said emphatically, "only I guess old Patch wouldn't stand for it."

"Hush, you mustn't say such things. He'll not be so bad as all that when he gets into our ways. Anyway, maybe Buster won't take him on."

"He'll take him on, you'll see."

And Buster did take Norman on: he was desperate for the extra help. Norman went back to Canoe later in the afternoon, having arranged to start work the very next morning and row over every day. "It's only for the school holiday," said Buster. "Kid's only fourteen, we mustn't forget that. He's had no sort of a home for a good upbringing. He'll improve; I'm only taking him on trial for the first week." Then Buster's eyes twinkled. "I guess a spot of work'll do him good," he said.

CHAPTER THIRTY-TWO

The following morning, in spite of my fifteen hours of work, I was up at four- fifteen, and out in the strawberry-bed by four-thirty. Eighteen one-pint containers had to be filled with sorted and shucked strawberries by breakfast time, so that Jessie could take them over on the ferry and put them in the frozen food locker.

These frozen food lockers are very popular in Canada, and are a great boon to people who have no refrigerators. Lockers of various sizes may be rented in refrigeration plants in most towns; the Harolds had one in Salmon Arm and saved themselves a good deal of money by storing meat there in quantity. They would slaughter their own pig and buy half a bullock or cow carcass; and they would pay the butcher to joint the meat for them, and to wrap and label each cut. All the packages were put in the locker, and presto! beef, pork, bacon and ham supplies for the year.

This year the Harolds wished to try preserving their strawberries in the same way.

Jessie had bought waxed cardboard containers specially designed for the purpose, with screw tops.

"My husband was given some frozen strawberries in hospital last winter," said Mrs. Harold. "He was in hospital for a week, you know, after a heart attack. He said you wouldn't have known them from fresh-picked ones. Strawberries in February – he couldn't believe his eyes at first! He came back here and talked about these strawberries so much that Jessie found out how they were done and bought the same kind of containers. Jes' fancy us having strawberry shortcake at Christmas!"

"They tell you how to do it on the containers," said Jessie. "You're supposed to pick only really good ones, no slugholes or little withered bits on them, or anything like that. And they have to be put in the freezer the same day they're picked, as soon as possible."

So, in order that the Harold family might enjoy their strawberry shortcake at Christmas, I had volunteered to get up at this fantastic hour and help Buster with the picking. He joined me a five, and we worked together for an hour. I always used to associate this particular job with headaches and broiling sun, and would have found it a pleasant change to do it in the cool of the morning, if only it had not been for the mosquitoes. I had not calculated for them, for during the day they mostly kept in the shade and near water, and only appeared at dusk. But all last night's mosquitoes seemed to have slept in the dew-laden strawberry plants. Swarms of them rose up from every plant we touched, and I was dreadfully bitten on my neck and wrists and legs, in spite of my habitual aura of insect repellent. I kept tucking my jeans into my socks, but both jeans and socks were too short, and in any case the mosquitoes could perfectly well bite through socks. Buster did not seem to be worried by them at all. "Funny thing," he said, "they always seem to go for a newcomer to the country. Canadian skittas get tired of Canadian blood, I guess."

At six o'clock we brought our strawberries into the kitchen, and Jessie came and helped me shuck them while Buster went off to do his chores. By milking time I was quite weary, and by breakfast time I was positively aching with hunger, and feeling as if I had already done a whole day's work. But I had volunteered, so I just kept quiet and hoed zealously between the sugar beets all the morning.

After lunch, when I went over to my cabin to write a letter, I sat down on the edge of the bed. "I'll just relax for a moment first," I thought, and lay back across the bed with my feet still on the floor. An hour had gone by when I woke up to find myself in the same position, with Jessie tapping on the open door and telling me the dishes were ready for drying.

That afternoon I took the team to the far field and did the last rakings, and when I came back Buster sent me to have another long rest. "And them's orders," he said.

I took my shoes off and stretched out, luxuriously if somewhat guiltily, on my bed. Soon, I reached for a magazine, and was idly turning the pages when Buster came and asked if he could use the post drill. "Yes, do," I said. "I'm not sleeping or anything. I shall enjoy your company." But I had not expected Norman's company too. He appeared a minute later, and all the time Buster was using the drill he lolled against the door-post, watching. I wondered what he would think of my idleness, until I realized that he was no busier than I was. He had arrived at eight that morning, and had been following Buster around ever since: all the work he had done had been to carry the occasional bucket for Buster. Officially, Buster was "showing him the ropes," but whenever I saw them it struck me that Norman was doing most of the talking. At present he was assuring Buster that he knew plenty about this kind of drill, his father had had one.

"Did you know it was called a post drill?' said Buster, without looking up. "Never heard that name for it."

"What did you call it?"

Norman looked confused for a moment. "I guess Dad called it the big drill, or somep'n," he mumbled. Then, brightly changing the subject, "There goes Derek's boat past the point. Is it true what they say, his wife's having another kid?"

After a while Buster sent him off to fetch something from the house, and when the boy had gone he stopped drilling and grinned at me. "That lad's father never had any post drill, you bet," he said. "He's never seen one in his life before. Just can't help talking big."

At breakfast Norman had "talked big" about his father almost ad nauseam, and everyone except the Doctor had listened politely. But during the washing up Mrs. Harold had whispered to me: "His Dad, Mr. Lundy, had been in gaol three times. He used to be a miner in Nelson – Mr. Lundy did, I mean - and now he has a job in the saw-mill in Canoe. One slip, though, and they'll sack him from that. It's no wonder Norman has to try and make him sound like somebody. You can't blame the lad."

Dr. Harold was less tolerant. At breakfast he had refused to answer Norman's remarks, or, for that matter, to speak at all; and he had been so disgusted with the boy's table manners that he had been unable to eat. Before dinner Mrs. Harold tactfully changed Norman's place with mine, so that her husband at least did not have to have the boy next to him.

"We'll keep it that way, if you don't mind, Lavender," she said.

"Poor Lavender," said Buster. "I wish she didn't have to go on sitting next to him."

"At least she doesn't have to sit opposite him," said Jessie with feeling. "That's far worse. You'll get that pleasure now."

"I shall look at my dinner," said Buster.

"I never thought," said Dr. Harold, "that in my house we should have to eat with such a lout that we didn't know whether it was worse to sit opposite him or next to him."

"He'll learn," said Buster. "He'll be okay."

CHAPTER THIRTY-THREE

Although it was only Norman's second day with us, I was already working less for Buster and more for his mother. I had had an upside-down morning in the strawberry bed and a foot-weary afternoon in the kitchen, and was so heartily sick of strawberries that I had been glad even of the break of half an hour's hoeing. It was, therefore, in a holiday mood that I set out alone, at a quarter to five, after the cows.

They had gone west and were being particularly elusive: no signs of them up the logging trail, no signs in the orchard. No hoof prints, no sound of a bell. Eventually I found tracks running west through the bush, on a wild trail high up the mountainside, and followed them for three quarters of an hour before I realized they were stale ones. Then I decided to get down to the shore, and took the first branch trail I saw.

It was a tiny path, leading off half left from the main trail and slanting down gradually through the bush. It took me a long way west without getting anywhere near the lake, but old Patch seemed to know it, and led me on with great hurry and many an anxious backward glance.

"Okay, old man," I said, "I guess you know best."

We made detours round big fallen trees and jumped over little ones. Down steep places we ran and slithered in the pine-needles, and on the level we walked solemnly. Round corners we came cautiously, through thick branches we pushed bravely. I was very conscious of the fact that this was only a wild, wild game-trail, far from the farm and leading Heaven knew where. Perhaps it was unknown even to Jessie, perhaps I was the first white person ever to go there! The one comfort was that it did keep going downhill, so surely I must come to the lake in the end. So long as that happened I knew I should be all right: once one was on the shore one had only to follow it and it was bound to lead one home eventually. It looked at the moment, though, as if there would be a powerful long stretch of shore to follow: this trail bade fair to reach the Pacific coast before the lake.

Everywhere out of the tangled underbrush grew the slender saplings, and everywhere among the saplings rose the tall columns of spruce and hemlock, cedar and pine: they joined together in a network of fan-vaulting high overhead, stealing the sunshine for themselves. Below, in the cool pine-needle shade, squirrel and chipmunk, cougar and bear, mule-deer and coyote must somewhere be carrying on their various businesses; and the fallen tree-trunks blackened and softened in their own slow time.

The trail dwindled till I was afraid it would david out altogether. Young spruce and cedar sent dense green branches across our way, now from one side, now from the other, then from both, so that the top half of me swam in a rustling coniferous sea while my invisible feet felt their way along after an invisible dog. Now and again a briar would clutch at my clothes and rip my skin, at the same time confronting me with such a cascade of crimson flowers as turned my curse into a gasp of wonder.

I was so busy with the branches, and with trying to keep near the submerged panting noises that indicated Patch's whereabouts, that I never noticed the sunlight striking down between the spruce and hemlock tops from an ever-widening chink of clear sky.

I had no idea I was anywhere near a clearing until I came bursting right into it. It was quite a shock. From my world of cool, green pine-needles and black half-rotten stumps, I practically fell into a sunlit meadow. It was no more than half an acre in size – a three-cornered hole cut in the deep forest, with the sun beating down from the triangle of blue sky at the top, and the long grass standing thickly all across the triangle at the bottom. The air was all full of golden sunshine, the humming of bees and the heavy scent of syringa. A Swallowtail butterfly zigzagged past me, turned back, and came to rest on a stone at my feet. It closed its wings and spread them, closed them and spread them, in slow, gloating luxury.

Behind me the trees stood tall and shady, and on my right they went on growing up the steep mountainside. But if this was a hole in the forest it was very near the edge: I could see blue sky and a distant mountain outline through those trees on the far side of the triangle. Nothing but a rocky bluff hid the lake itself from view. I stood very still, and above the humming of the bees I could just hear the welcome sound of the water: slap-slap-slap, ssh, slap-slap-slap-slap.

Suddenly I recognized the meadow: I had come to it a long way around, but it was the same place where Jessie and I found the cows one evening over a month before, the time she had showed me the salt-lick. Alas, there was no sign of a cow this time, but the salt-lick would still be there: it was just the other side of that rocky bluff. I would go and have a proper look at it, for when Jessie had showed me I had been too tired to appreciate it.

I still remember the beauty of those tall grass flowers, the stupid hay-fever that they inspired, and the joy of finding a path right across, where by walking carefully I could avoid disturbing a single pollen-loaded head. I remember the sensation of uphill, of stones underfoot, and then, oh, then, down there between the trees, the lake! Blue water, sparkling water, rippling below the dark branches, spreading its serene loveliness away and away to the far shores. The dark outline of Merganser Point, stretched half across the lake to hide the foot of Spruce Hills. Canoe village, dwarfed by distance but recognisable by its yellow sawdust-pile and its long white wharf; and, behind and above all, deep blue and rust red, my dear, faithful Mount Ida. How I was growing to love that mountain!

One last glance at the hidden, sun-drenched meadow, and I moved on down a new kind of terrain. Nothing was there but bare rock, loose stones, and a scattering of withered grass over the dry earth. A few twisted pines grew miraculously out of the hard rock. Below me, crags tumbled down, steeper and perilously steeper till at last they dropped sheer, ending in a sharply chiselled line above the deep water.

I found the homeward path, which contoured around rough shoulders of rock and into stony gullies, and soon came upon the salt-lick. There was no recognizable salt there, only dry, powdery earth; but it must have been tasty earth, for in two or three places anxious animal feet had scraped and pawed at it, making strange dusty hollows back into the steep hillside. In the hollows, and all around them, the grey dust was pitted with deer-tracks. A network of narrow paths covered the hillside, converging on the hollows, and there were tracks on every path. Sharp little hoofs had trodden their way there, down from the bush, up from the shore, round the bluff from the meadow and along the old cow-trail from the east.

I searched in vain among the deer-tracks for signs of my cows. What a place this would be, I reflected, for watching game, it one had hours to spare. But I had not!

It was already almost two hours since I had left the house, and I had not even heard a cow-bell. I hurried along the trail, and soon the salt-lick was far behind and the tall hemlocks closed overhead. Old Patch ran ahead, puffing and smiling and anxious to be home, and Blackie, as usual stuck faithfully to my heels. We were all three of us tired.

Suddenly fatigue enveloped me and I felt very sorry for myself. I had had nothing to eat for six and half hours, the dogs were useless, and the terror of cougars and bears lurked on every high branch and behind every stump. I resolved to go home and confess failure; on the way I would seek the comfort of a word with the compassionate Birminghams. But at that moment I caught sight of an old cabin Jessie had once pointed out to me. It was empty now, but at least it had been a human habitation. I felt safe again, and the self-pity vanished: how gregarious one is, in spite of oneself! I planned to saunter up to the Birminghams' place, shout to Mrs. Birmingham, "Hello there! You haven't seen our cows around here, have you?" Then, shrugging my shoulders, "Oh well. I 'spect I'll find them up the logging road," and I would stride casually off up the trail.

But that was not the way things turned out, at all. In less than twenty minutes I found myself sitting in the sun in front of the cabin, the object of much fuss and sympathy. Mrs. Birmingham brought me out a mug of hot tea, listened to the details of my fruitless search, and registered horror when I told her I had been out for two and half hours. The mixture of tea and sympathetic concern made me feel very brave and energetic, but Mrs. Birmingham would not hear of my going any further, not without help. "David will help you," she said. "He went out fishing, but he'll be back any minute now. I know he'll be glad to help." She was very insistent, so I waited.

Soon the rowboat appeared round the point and crept towards us across the bay. David landed, pulled the boat up onto the stones, and grasped the situation in an instant. He was quicker than I. Before I had grasped anything, he had vanished into the bush, and a whole plan of campaign had been worked out. I was to stay put. If he found the cows within half an hour, he would signal from a certain point along the shore; if not, he would work his way eastwards and meet me at the Cookes' house.

As the Cookes' house was on the far side of the next bay, I gladly accepted Mrs. Birmingham's offer of her rowboat. Half an hour passed slowly, with no signal from David. I felt somewhat guilty about handing over my job in this way, and the dogs did not ease my conscience at all, whining all the time and gazing mournfully at me. They made me feel perfectly dreadful. I was glad when the time came for me to bundle them into the little blue boat and push off from the pebbly beach.

I had expected trouble from the dogs, but I need not have worried, for they knew all about boats: Blackie lay down on the boards behind me, and Patch sat in the stern by my feet.

The cabin dwindled away before my eyes till it was a mere speck beyond the shining ripples; while above it the green points of the firs rose behind one another, tier upon tier, till they cut a serrated line against the sky. I was blissfully happy to be rowing again. I was happy with the muscular effort of pulling the oars through the water; happy with the delicate thrill in the hands, and the whispered skutter-putter-putter, as the blades skimmed back over the ripples for the next stroke; I was happy with the speed, the dwindling of the cabin on the shore, and the rhythm of sound and motion. A long- forgotten song ran through my mind, a carefree, lilting jingle which we used to sing as a round at school:

"Row, row, row your boat

Gently down the stream,

Merrily, merrily, merrily, merrily, Life is but a dream."

What a dream, indeed! When I considered that I, my ordinary, English, buttered- toast-eating self, was rowing on Shuswap Lake in the heart of B.C.'s forested mountains, with a sheepdog and a spaniel for passengers; and that my job was to retrieve a herd of Jersey cattle from somewhere in that gigantic landscape – well! It seemed inevitable that I should soon wake up. But, instead of waking in a comfortable bed, I found myself getting into an increasingly uncomfortable part of the lake. As I pulled out from the shelter of the bay to round the headland, I came slap into a head wind. The boat bobbed up and down frantically, and I had difficulty in making any headway at all. The song in my mind changed to a more appropriate one, with extra slow temp:

"Yo-o, HEAVE, ho;

Yo-o, HEAVE, ho;

Pom, pom, tid-del-y pom,

Yo-o, HEAVE, ho."

To make matters worse, Patch stood up and placed himself just where my hands would biff him on the head every time they came forwards. I could not alter my stroke, and nothing would induce Patch to sit down or move away; so I continued, mercilessly, with my rowing. Sometimes he would turn his head away and my hand would miss it, but then he would turn back and get hit again, biff, biff, biff. Poor old boy, he looked so pained and insulted! But there was nothing I could do about it, apologies and threats were equally useless.

Somehow I pulled round that point, but in the second bay the wind and waves were coming at me sideways, and I did a great deal of inexpert zig-zagging before I reached calm water below the Cookes'. I had a nasty feeling that critical eyes were upon me, and I determined to prove that, whatever my steering was like, at least I could make an expert landing.

I was lucky. Mr. and Mrs. Cooke came down to their garden gate and chatted with me for a while. "Ah, so it is you!" said Mrs. Cooke. "We thought it must have been Jessie till we saw you only had the two dogs. Jessie always takes the new little bitch along too, doesn't she?" So they had thought I was Jessie: that was sure proof that my steering had not been so bad. As for my landing, that was paid the supreme compliment of being taken for granted.

The Cookes had seen nothing of David: I went along the shore to the big clearing below the logging road, and settled down to wait for him there. It was a point of vantage, for from it I could see the whole bay, the little blue boat below the Cookes' gate, and every point on the shore where David would be likely to come out; and I could also see up a hundred yards of clearing to the bottom of the logging road.

I sat down on a log at the edge of the trees and enjoyed the warm sun. The dogs drank noisily from the lake, and came to sit near me, dripping and smiling and panting.

I looked at my watch: eight o'clock, and David had begun his search at seven. He should be here any minute now. I kept scanning the shore, and now and again I glanced up the clearing. No David. Five past eight came, and ten past, and twenty past. Still no David. I began to think sad thoughts about supper. Even if David appeared now with the cows it would take us half an hour to get them home, half an hour to wait while they got dry from the creek, and a third half-hour to milk them: supper at ten minutes to ten at the earliest. When one had had lunch at twelve, that seems like a long time to wait for the next meal.... The sad thoughts grew too sad, and had to be suppressed.

I stared out across the water. The sun was slipping down the western sky towards the steep firred mountainside, and the evening mosquitoes began to shrill past my ears. I slapped angrily at my arms, and unrolled my jeans to protect my ankles. Half past eight, and still no David. Driven by mosquitoes and the fear of darkness, I got up, left a message with Mrs. Cooke for David, and began the long slow climb up the logging road alone.

Up and up we went, I and the two reluctant dogs. We halted for a moment on the open corner where one could look out over the canyon tree-tops and get a bird's eye view of the Harolds' hay meadow, with its irrigation ditches marked clear and its apple- trees looking like little, round cushions. A band of trees made it a dark frame on the far side, separating its small tidiness from a wild splendour of mountains and shining water. I turned and plodded on once more up the trail.

On my right, feathery cedar branches concealed the steep drop to the canyon's edge, and the deep roar of the falls grew louder and louder with every step I took. Soon it was crashing about my ears like thunder; and the green branches and all the air between shook with the many voices of the water.

It had always been a joy to me to hear that great singing of the waters, and to feel the thunder of it pulsing in my veins; but this day there was fear, too – a fear which intensified the joy, merged with it, and finally overwhelmed it, so that the singing of terror in my ears distorted the song of the waters. Deep in my heart were sensuous, almost pleasurable fears: of the waters' symphony, of the thick, breathing greenness around me, of the high mountains, and of the titanic forests beneath whose stems I crept like an ant, minute and helpless. But in my throat, clutching like a cold hand, was the old dread of bears.

The trail levelled out and dwindled to a grassy path, and dense bushes closed in around me – blinkers for me, safe hiding for the bears. I felt blind but horribly visible. A little patch left the trail on my left and disappeared into a tangle of under-brush: I felt the goose flesh down my back and the sweat on my hands before I remembered that this was the path which had led me to my previous encounter with Bruin. When I came to the place by the canyon head where the water rang like bells to baffle searchers for cows, and where the young cedars joined hands across the hidden trail for twenty paces, I gave in. I could not face the blind plunge through those cedars. Why, there might be a bear waiting for me in the clearing at the other end!

More likely, the cows were waiting there, but for all I cared they could wait till Kingdom Come. Home for me, and quickly, too, before nightfall. Home to food, rest, friends and safety.

I went back down that logging trail on the run, though goodness knows where the energy came from. Back past the ill-fated little path; past cedar and spruce, spruce and cedar; down and down, past trees and rocks and ferns. Down to the open corner for a brief glimpse of the meadow, grey with sleep beneath the solemn trees. Away on down, into the silence of the forest, till the crashing choral symphony of the water died away to a hushing whisper. Past the top of the Cookes' steep garden, through the junipers in the clearing. Into the bush again, out onto the shore, over the creek bridge.

Night came, and at last I was threading my way between the trees on the Harolds' beach. It was good to be back, but I did not look forward to facing Buster and Jessie. I hated admitting failure. What was far worse, I knew that Jessie, worried, tired and resigned, would herself set off into the night to do the job which I had failed to do. Poor tired Jessie, going up the mountains in the dark, and probably going without the dogs because I, Lavender, had exhausted them already. Oh, dear!

As I came through the gate I saw a light in the cow-barn: Buster would be there, feeding the horses maybe. I would go straight to him – anything to put off facing Jessie! I cut across the meadow and went round the side of the house, stumbling in the darkness as I made for that welcome square of soft, flickering light. For a moment I had a strange feeling that I had been wasting my time, that – but no, it was too much to hope for, I must not think it.

But yes! It was true! I could hear the clink of a bucket, the murmur of low voices, the pinging of milk into the pail. And when I came to the doorway, there was the hurricane lamp hanging from a beam, and the cows' tails swishing in the shadowy stalls, and Buster milking Jenny as calm as you please.

It was impossible. I must be suffering from delusions. I leaned my head against the doorpost and closed my eyes for a moment; but when I opened them again the cows were still there.

"Oh, Buster!" I said.

"We got your cows for you," said Buster with infinite kindness.

"Oh." Tears of relief stung at the backs of my eyes, but I fought them back. Then Norman came slouching up, bucket in hand, and grinned at me.

"Cows came down back of the meadow half an hour ago," he said. "Jessie and I fetched 'em in." He looked at me with a superior and faintly amused tolerance, as if he had been managing the entire farm while I indulged in a ladylike walk in the woods. Suddenly I hated the sight of him, and escaped into the house.

Two hours later I was in my cabin, undressing by the flickering light of the oil-lamp and thinking how kind everybody had been. I had not been allowed to do any more chores, and before I ate my supper Jessie had insisted on my drinking a glass of cherry wine. Wonderful stuff! It wakened my appetite, drove away the stinging tears from the backs of my eyes, and made me glow inside with its own red warmth. It was first class wine, and twenty-four years old; Jessie and her mother had made it themselves, and it was brought out only on the most special occasions. I was much honoured that this one was considered special enough.

Yes it was pretty special: those cows had been known to come home on their own perhaps twice in a summer, and here they were doing it for me a second time within a few weeks. First, they had come when I could not face that bear, and now, when I shrank from the night in the bush.

If the cows had saved me from an awkward situation and the Harolds had been considerate, perhaps the kindest of all had been David. For hours he must have searched for those cows before going back to his boat, and yet even then he did not go straight home. He came walking right round to Harolds', arriving after ten o'clock at night, simply to "see that Lavender was okay."

CHAPTER THIRTY-FOUR

Next morning I rose at six-thirty as usual, and milked in a kind of stupor. When I had unchained the cows I went up to Buster, stifling a yawn.

"Which way shall I put the bossies, Buster?"

"Let's see, it's Saturday, isn't it? Better put 'em west, please, Lavender; they'll have to go east tomorrow."

"Okay," said I, but my heart sank. I knew well that they always went west on a Saturday, but I had just hoped.... Oh, well, maybe they would not go far, not on two days running. I took them along the beach, drove them into the water and stood watching until they were all assembled on the far side of the creek. "Please, bossies, oh please be somewhere near and safe this evening," I entreated them silently. And all day long, as I washed dishes and hoed sugar beets, I tried to will those cows to stay near home. I dreaded a repetition of yesterday's adventure.

But I need not have worried, for my wishes were more than granted, though in an unexpected way. In the afternoon clouds piled up, and at about four o'clock a light rain began to fall. It came on to rain steadily, and poured all that evening.

At a quarter to five I finished hoeing and came to the house to look for the dogs. Buster was bending over the cold frame by the hen-run; he straightened up and called to me as I went by. Buster in the rain was an amazing sight. He was wearing a torn, shiny waterproof, and had pulled a shapeless gaberdine hat well down onto his head. Locks of his wild hair had managed to escape from under the dripping hat, and he had a good week's growth of beard.

"What a villainous exterior," I thought, "for the gentlest person I know." I went over the him.

"I want to get these cabbages in while it's wet," he said, digging another one out of the frame and putting it beside its companions in a bucket. "Do you think you could help me with them?"

"Well, yes," I said, "but -"

"Oh, you don't have to think about the cows. I asked Jes, and she'll be fetching them herself today."

So I had a wet but safe time planting cabbages with Buster. Although the job took us less than an hour, Jessie appeared in the kitchen with the dogs before we had finished washing our earthy hands. "I've put the cows straight into the barn," she announced. "They were only just beyond Cooke's, in the old orchard."

As it happened, I never had to fetch the cows again – not on my own. I went once more with Jessie, but on other evenings she fetched them alone, because she particularly wanted to train the new bitch, Tess, herself.

One day Buster sent Norman on the job. "He's got to learn sometimes," he said. Norman went striding off, very self-confident, Patch following a long way behind with many a backward glance. Jessie had to hide till they were both out of sight, lest the dog run back to her.

"He'll have to manage on his own," said Buster. "That dog will never work for him."

"Do him good," said Dr. Harold. "Get some of his fat down."

"I hope the boy won't get lost," said Mrs. Harold. "Do you think he'll be all right, Buzz?"

"Sure, he'll be okay. I'm worried he'll upset the cows when he does find them, though; and that

he'll bring them back on the run. He's so noisy and rough, he scares them."

But an hour later we heard the bells coming along the shore, and both Norman and the cows turned up, orderly and unruffled.

Personally I believe Buster was a little disappointed, though he was the first to give Norman a word of praise.

Buster was wonderful with that boy. He was tolerant and infinitely patient. Norman adored him and continued to follow him everywhere: Mrs. Harold and Jessie called him "Buster's new shadow;" but Buster called him "my elephant" - only behind his back, of course, but never maliciously, sometimes even tenderly. Buster's sense of humour never left him: when Norman had been particularly maddening he would merely shrug his shoulders and grin secretly at me. He would let Norman do jobs in his own way, only offering advice gradually and judiciously, and only interfering if disaster threatened. "Let him learn for himself," he was always saying.

Even the time Norman got the stone-boat jammed in a wire fence and then confused the horse with contrary orders, Buster gave him a few minutes' chance to get out of the mess himself. Not until he saw Duke was becoming really frightened did he step forward. "Just you stand here a minute, Norman," he said. He spoke quietly to Duke, unhitched him, and led him round to the other end of the stone-boat where he hitched him on again. "Now lead him out, and keep that voice down," he said.

But the trouble with Norman was, not so much that he went about jobs in the wrong way, as that he avoided them wherever and whenever possible. The moment Buster left him doing a job on his own he would slow up and stop, coming into the kitchen for a drink and chattering to whoever was there, or just sitting down on a log "having a breather." These "breathers" would last until Buster came into view. Buster used to leave him to bring in wood to pile in the kitchen, and to chop more outside. Now the Harold idea was to chop enough wood to make a pile four or five feet high in the corner by the stove, and when that was all brought in, to chop more and more and yet more, whenever one had a few minutes to spare. But Norman, who had a whole morning for it and might have done enough to make wood-chopping unnecessary for a week, would bring in a couple of armfuls and then give up.

"Gee, I'm sweating like a pig," he'd say.

Buster, who had never slacked off in his life and hated laziness as much as did the rest of his family, saw red. But he kept his temper, and used only polite suggestions and mild sarcasm, both of which rolled off Norman's thick skin like water off the proverbial duck's back. "Buzz is too gentle with him," complained Mrs. Harold; but Norman was Buster's property and she would not have dreamt of interfering.

Norman's curiosity was insatiable. He was forever prying into other people's affairs and loved talking scandal; but what he liked best of all was to watch other people work. Although the harvest was in, David still continued to come on most days. He was helping Buster saw the timber for the new house, and the two of them worked for hours on end sawing planks from enormous tree-trunks with the saw-carriage, another ingenious contraption of Harold design and manufacture.

Norman, fascinated by the work, and by the little spitting petrol-engine that worked the machine, left his woodpile and slouched across the yard. He stood, hands in pockets and mouth agape, blatantly watching, and occasionally flinging some blasé remark at David.

The first time this happened Buster said nothing. "Let the kid have a good stare," was his attitude, "then he won't be interested anymore." But when the same thing had occurred three mornings running, Norman always wandering across from his work only half an hour after being sent back to it, Buster got really angry. That afternoon he took Norman off somewhere and gave him what must have been, even by less gentle standards than Buster's, a real dressing down. Anyway, it was remarkably effective: Norman became almost conscientious in his work from that day forth. Laziness was still part of his temperament, but at least he tried to overcome it; and he developed a healthy respect for Buster, whom he adored more than ever. He noticed Buster's ways with animals and made an effort to copy them: towards the end of the week he was beginning to be quite quiet and gentle with them.

Norman's language around the cow-barn infuriated me, but I followed Buster's example and tried to ignore it. "He'll learn," Buster said, "he'll learn." He would, too. I felt sure that, under Buster's influence, he would even become a likeable person.

CHAPTER THIRTY-FIVE

During my last week at the Harolds' I worked as hard as ever. In fact on one day, Wednesday, I did my hardest job yet: removing last winter's entire muck-heap from the cow-barn alley way and spreading it in the berry patch. I commandeered Duke, the stone-boat and a long fork, and did everything myself. I piled the muck into the stone-boat and drove, standing on top of it, away across the bumpity fields and over the irrigation ditches; then I unloaded it, forkful by forkful, directly onto the loganberry roots. There were three big loads, and it took me the whole day. I ached and dripped in the intense heat, and my shoes must have smelt abominable, but I was sun-tanned and exhilarated, and inordinately proud of myself.

Buster was grateful to have the job done at last, and said some very complimentary things to me afterwards, but it had not been his idea that I should do it: indeed, I had had to use a great deal of persuasion before he would let me. "It's much too hard for a girl," he said, "and I don't think it's a nice job for you at all." Nor did the rest of the family: such was their opinion of muck that they could not bring themselves to call it muck, or even manure, but always referred to it as "fertilizer." Now I call it muck, and I like working with it. I even like the smell of it – though I refrained from telling the Harolds that. But on this occasion I had additional reasons for wanting such a job: I longed to do something more responsible than weeding or strawberry picking, something more complete in itself; and, above all, I wanted to do something big for Buster. I had to prove myself worthy of him, to repay him in some measure for his kindness to me. I felt rather guilty about leaving the

Harolds: it may have been stupid, with Norman here, to feel I was letting them down, but I did feel that, so I tried to make it up to them by hard work.

Perhaps, too, I was a little jealous of Norman? I do not know. Certainly all that week, though I must have done as much work as ever, I remember feeling that he was already replacing

me, and that I was somehow not as necessary as before. I threw myself into all my labours, trying to prove that thoroughness and zest were worth more than mere male strength.

For my reward I had Buster's open approval, which meant a lot to me; also the unexpected relief, recurring daily, of not having to fetch the cows any more. To make matters even better, I was having a succession of outings. Now that the general strain of haymaking was over, there was a feeling of cheerful relaxation in the air. The Harolds, for once, were not tired. Jessie was expecting a friend to stay at the weekend, and was as excited as a schoolgirl before half-term. Buster, having three able-bodied helpers (David still came nearly every day), was hard put to it to find enough jobs for us all. The family had the rare satisfaction of being well ahead with their work; and they all caught Jessie's gaiety. It seemed to me to be a week of holidays.

It all began with the photographs on Sunday.

Sundays always felt like holidays and this one was no exception. The simpler and rarer one's pleasures, the more intensely can one enjoy them, and it was with a sense of tremendous luxury that I rolled out of bed as late as seven-thirty. I revelled in milking an hour late, and settled happily down to a nine o'clock breakfast accompanied by the B.B.C. commentary from home. After breakfast Norman rowed himself home to Canoe for his day off, and I am afraid everyone heaved a guilty but audible sigh of relief. Our holiday spirits soared even higher, and remained soaring in spite of the work.

For there was work. The family were expecting guests to lunch, and we all worked hard preparing for them. It was to be a very special lunch. Jessie gathered vegetables and retired to the kitchen to spend ages washing and peeling them, while Buster, Mrs. Harold and I all picked strawberries for another of the famous strawberry shortcakes. When the strawberries were done I was landed with my most hated job, washing the separator; but for once I hardly noticed what I was doing, there was such an air of festivity in the kitchen.

In the end a superb meal was ready: a huge joint of beef, new potatoes, young carrots, young sugar beet thinnings and rich brown gravy; and a gigantic and perfect strawberry shortcake supplemented by a spare platter full of strawberries.

But no guests!

All the morning the wind had been blowing gustily, sending fitful showers before it. "Bad storms whip up on the lake so quickly," said Buster. "Perhaps they won't come."

If the guests did come the Harolds would want to entertain them in the house all the afternoon; but if they could not face the lake, then neither could we. "Poor Lavender," said Buster. "Her last Sunday and no boat trip, it's too bad." But I was too happy to mind that. Happiness was in the air.

The visitors never did turn up. Mrs. Harold gave them until one o'clock then dished up the feast. She must have been disappointed, so must they all, but the whole family took things in good heart: they were used to the capriciousness of their lake. We had the radio on and listened to the last half of the usual church service while we ate. There was the very best kind of Harold Atmosphere, as I called it to myself: a peacefulness we had missed at meals since Norman had come. I realized for the first time that this was the only house where I did not mind the combination of church worship and eating. The Harolds could preserve an atmosphere of reverence in which there was no trace of awkwardness or constraint. With them, it did not seem odd at all to be helping oneself to vegetables in the middle of the Lord's Prayer. Give us this day our daily bread. Why should it seem odd, indeed?

We were so late with lunch that the service ended as we were finishing the meat course, and Buster switched off the radio. Jessie and I cleared the plates out and Mrs. Harold brought in the strawberry shortcake. She sat, spoon in hand, and beamed round at us all. "Well," she said, "it's an extra large one, for seven, and we're only five. I guess we'll all have to eat plenty."

All eyes were on the dish. "Suits me," said Buster. "And me," said Jessie.

"And me," said I.

Dr. Harold only grinned. He was not a big eater, which was hardly surprising, considering he was over eighty and refused to wear his false teeth.

We all ate big helpings, and we all (except the Doctor) passed our plates up for more, and the shortcake was exactly finished. There was nothing left but half a dozen strawberries and a few spoonfuls of juice, on the "spare" platter. It was inconceivable to the Harolds that one dish could be made to last for more than one meal.

Just as we were picking up our spoons and forks to begin again, in walked David. We all looked at each other and burst out laughing. David looked puzzled for a moment, then quickly saw the point.

"You been having strawberry shortcake again?" he said. "Well, isn't that just my darnedest luck!"

"Here, Dave, you have mine!"

"No, have mine!"

"No, mine!

We began holding up our plates, but Jessie rushed to the cupboard and got an extra one. "We'll all give him some," she said, and began passing the plate round the table. By the time we had each contributed from our second helpings, David's plate contained at least as much as a first and a second helping together. He blushed and laughed and tried to stop us, but we made him sit down, and once he had got it before him he ate it all willingly enough.

Mrs. Harold winked at me. "Bet he came over jest for the shortcake," she said.

"They all do."

David rose to the bait and we all teased him mercilessly. Our hilarity continued throughout the washing up, and after that, as it was wet outside, we spent the afternoon round the living-room table looking at all the family photograph albums.

It was an absorbing occupation. I do not know who enjoyed it the most, David and I being shown, or the Harolds proudly showing. They certainly had a varied collection. There were faded old sepia enlargements of Dr. and Mrs. Harold's wedding photographs, in an envelope. There were some lovely pictures taken recently by Buster – results of his sense of beauty as well as of a certain amount of good luck – pictures of the canyon falls, of lake water undulating away from the stern of a boat, of hoar frost on wire netting. There were family groups with Buster and Jessie as small or larger children, groups of friends David and I had not seen, snapshots of Patch as a puppy, of Jessie with previous dogs, and of various members of the family gardening or harvesting in earlier years.

These old photographs fascinated me. Dr Harold in his youth had had, it appeared, dark flashing eyes and a large moustache. The Buster of twenty years ago had been, to my intense delight, strikingly good-looking: it was not hard to imagine myself falling for him, and it occurred to me that I should like to have been born twenty years earlier.... A pang of hunger shot through me: why was David not somehow different, or Buster younger?

But there was no time for romantic ideas; we had more to see, and yet more.

With pride we were shown pictures of the Harolds' corn crop at maturity, a palmy avenue growing high above Buster's head (the corn I had planted was but a few inches high now, I could hardly believe it would grow so tall). "We always grow heralded crops," said the Doctor, and shook with laughter at his own joke. With another kind of pride Buster showed us proof of a certain terrible storm he had told me about: two snaps of a mountain slope beyond Fortress Mountain, with the trees fallen this way and that like trampled wheat, a jumbled desolation of matchwood with one or two thin saplings rising from its midst and a

Lilliputian man sitting on one of the matchsticks in the foreground.

When at last we had seen everything, and Jessie and Buster were beginning to tidy up, we found to our surprise that the sun was shining and the wind had dropped. It was then that David invited me to tea.

"Oh, David, I'd love to, but I don't know if – there's the milking, you see.

I -" "I'll ask Buster. Buster, you'd let me take your farmerette out to tea, wouldn't you? Please?"

"We-ell," drawled Buster, putting his head on one side in mock consideration,

"I think you might -".

"You see, I thought she might catch her first fish on the way over; I've brought my rod and tackle."

"Of course you can take her! She should have had a boat trip with us today, by rights." He smiled at me. "I wouldn't want Lavender to leave us without catching any fish at all. They just don't seem to come to her when she's in our boat; perhaps they will in yours."

"I'll see she catches something," David said; and my fate was settled for me. We both thanked Buster and set off right away, to have more time for the fishing.

I do not recollect the details of that visit: I only know that I revelled in the rest, the change, and the opportunity to talk about the Harolds instead of to them.

But I certainly remember my first fish: for I did catch it. David (unnecessarily, I thought, but I was uninitiated in the mysteries of fishing) kept making me reel in my line so that he could try yet another bait on it for me. He had a strange assortment of objects called spoons and plugs which looked to me more like broken propellers and badly-made toy fishes; in the end one of these oddities attracted something, and there came a tug on my line. I almost fell overboard in my excitement, and reeled in, expecting something enormous. My voice rose to a squeak: "Oh, David, I've got something!"

All my own work 10- 1/2 oz.

When my victim came flapping to the surface I almost burst with pride. It was a Kamloops trout, and it only weighed eleven and a half ounces, which was considered a mere trifle on Shuswap Lake, but it was as good as a twenty-pounder to me. When Mrs. Birmingham weighed it David wanted to put stones in its mouth to improve matters, but I would have none of that. The only concession I made to him was when we got back to the Harolds' at sunset. I hid the fish behind my back, and when Buster asked how much it weighed I said: "Eleven and a half."

"Eleven and a half pounds?"

"No, only ounces, I'm afraid."

There were roars of laughter all round.

Mrs. Harold fried my fish for me next morning, for my own exclusive breakfast.

It was just the right size for me, and I swear it was the best fish I had ever tasted. There is no better recipe for fish than to catch your own.

Before David went home that night he invited us all to come to tea the next day, including Norman; so on Monday there was another outing. At three o'clock we all stopped work; everybody changed, Buster shaved his father while Mrs. Harold cut his hair, and we all set off in the boat at four, feeling immensely respectable. We had a grand party on the Birminghams' verandah, and, thanks to Buster's outboard motor, did not have to hurry away. People of leisure!

We were back by six-fifteen, when, to make everything perfect, we found the cows considerately waiting by the north gate of their own meadow, not a hundred yards from the barn.

I was due to leave on Thursday, for that was the day the ferry-boat came. Tuesday passed without special event to mark it, and the fateful day drew near. I was divided in my feelings about leaving. Something in me, something undefined but strong never the less, made me long passionately for Thursday, almost counting the hours to the time of my departure: I had to go on from here. Whatever had first driven me across Canada to Salmon Arm was driving me once again: "It is time," it said, "go on, go on." Where to, and why? Geographically, I know the answers: I must go to the Coast, I must cover the last three hundred miles of the journey, go down the Fraser Canyon, see Vancouver, see the Pacific Ocean at last. But spiritually where was I going, and to what purpose? I did not know.

Sometimes I thought I knew, but nothing was clear to me yet. The strange force that moved me – Fate, if you will - brooked no refusal. Yet even while I longed to comply with it, I hated the prospect it offered, the prospect of leaving these dear people whom I had grown to love and who needed my help; I dreaded the day when I should have to step back from their world into my own, from their gentle discipline into the harsh complexities of modern life outside. So it was with an odd mixture of long suffering and relief that I let myself be persuaded to stay on over the weekend.

"Must you go tomorrow?" asked Buster, after lunch on Wednesday. "Couldn't you just stay till Monday?"

"We would so like you to meet Frances," pleaded Jessie. Frances was the friend who was coming to

stay. "She's a woodsy person like yourself, loves everything out-of- doors. I know you'd like her; and I've told her so much about you in letters, she's all set to meet you now."

"Frances sure would be disappointed if she missed you," said Buster. "Besides, we never work much when she's here, she only comes once a year. We'll be going all kinds of places – won't we Jess? Up to Mosquito Creek, maybe. We want you to enjoy the fun too. Just one little weekend more, it can't make much difference to you. Please stay!

When I reminded them about the ferry-boat only going on Thursdays, Buster said: "Oh, but you don't need to worry about that. I'll take you to Canoe on Monday."

"We'll be taking Frances over anyway," said Jessie. "We could take you and her both. Oh, you will stay, won't you?"

What could I do? I promised to stay till Monday, of course; and I went on with my muck-carting.

That night, after the milking, we left the pails to be washed later, and listened to a broadcast by the Glasgow Orpheus Choir. Buster lay back in his easy chair and slept, Patch at his feet and Tess stretched adoringly up him from his knees to his chest, her pointed nose resting under his chin. I relaxed in another armchair opposite him; Jessie, Mrs. Harold and David sat at the table, abstractedly drinking glasses of milk; and the Doctor was behind the curtains, in bed. We were all at peace together. Tired backs and arms were at rest, busy hands still. The music filled the air and brought peace to our inmost selves. The singing danced and dreamed and soared, and our minds were free to dance and dream and soar with it. For a while I closed my eyes, and then all the world was kept at bay, shut out – all but the music, and that came inside me, swelling my heart and pulsing through my veins, lifting me high, high above myself. At the end of a song it set me gently down, but the peace was unbroken.

A new song began, and my eyes were open again and resting on Buster's sleeping face. All at once my heart melted within me. I let my gaze travel down over the place where his plaid shirt sagged in because of the missing ribs, over his forearms where the great muscles and strong tendons showed beneath the suntanned skin, and over his broad hands, mutilated but undefeated, which rested caressingly on the sleeping dog; and I knew I loved him.

But my love for Buster was not the attraction of one adult towards another. It was somewhat akin to the love I used to feel, as a child, for the Christ of the hymn-book pictures: an aching tenderness in which my passion for the eyes, the hands, the kindly beard and tortured human body, and my longing for physical nearness to these things, were inextricably mixed with an abstract love of the Good, the True and the Beautiful. I did not think of my emotions in this light at the time, but that was the way they were.

I felt a deep respect for the selflessness and humility, the strength of will and the superb courage which were all carried, in Buster, to a degree beyond my imagining; and while my tenderness would have had me run and lay my head on his knees, my respect kept me at a reverent distance. I was content that this should be so. Buster's virtues were angelic in my sight, and one does not have romantic notions about angels.

Suddenly my eyes were caught by a glint of light off David's glasses and I knew he had been watching me. Poor David! He had been having romantic notions: he had tried to make love to me in the kitchen that very evening, and I had laughingly rebuffed him. Now he was gazing straight ahead of him with a look of such profound sadness that I felt ashamed of my cruelty. Perhaps he thought I was in love with Buster? Oh, but he was wrong, he didn't understand. Perhaps he was even falling in love with me! I dismissed this idea as absurd, impossible. For myself, I seemed just now to be strangely immune from emotional entanglements. I would find them elsewhere, maybe, but not here. This was not the right place, not the right time.

CHAPTER THIRTY-SIX

Frances came on the ferry-boat next evening, and there was rejoicing in the Harold household. There were kisses and handshakes, compliments and questions, laughter and reminiscences. There was a triumphal strawberry shortcake for supper, and even a glass of the precious cherry wine for everybody. The Harolds were in great form; obviously they all loved Frances and she loved all of them.

Frances was the same age as Jessie, but as different from her as a ladybird from a daddy-long legs.

She was plump and dumpy, and her greying hair was short, thick and frizzy. She had a round,

smiling face, twinkling black eyes, and a complexion that would have been the envy of any schoolgirl. She was quick and cheerful, and seemed to bounce about everywhere like an indian rubber ball; yet she remembered and respected the Harolds' slow and thorough little habits, and assisted at their washing up without doing a thing wrong, or appearing to find their methods any different from her own. And, although it was over a year since she had visited the place, she remembered exactly where every cup, plate and saucepan belonged.

Jessie shared her bedroom with Frances, and the two of them went everywhere together – even to the house in the garden, where they could go on talking through the partition.

Jessie could talk to her heart's content about the local news – especially about the births, deaths, marriages and newcomers – for Frances was anxious to hear it all. Frances had once lived in Canoe, but now, unfortunately for Jessie, she had a job in New Westminster, right away down on the Coast. Their friendship was a deeper one than Jessie had with any of the "neighbours" whom she met on Thursdays and Sundays: it was evidently something very important in her life. No wonder, I thought, she had looked forward so intensely to her friend's arrival.

It was not hard to see why they all loved Frances. I liked her at once: she was such a happy, unselfish little person. She helped delightedly in all the chores from milking to dish washing, admired every plant Buster showed her in the garden and talked for hours with the two old people. She came with genuine enthusiasm on every expedition, including, one morning, the ritual journey up the canyon with Buster and Jessie. Frances enjoyed every single thing the Harolds enjoyed, and even more so, because she had to spend most of her time in a dreary city office.

It was true, what Buster had said about not doing much work during Frances's visit. We had no less than three outings on my three last days.

On the Friday evening Frances, Jessie, Buster and I went to visit the Lesters across the bay, having milked early and changed into our Sunday best after supper. That afternoon I had already been called away from work for half an hour to join the others in listening to another radio concert.

On Saturday I picked strawberries for the last time (the crop was nearly over); and I spent my last working afternoon puffing Derris dust onto some young turnip plants with a large and clumsy hand-pump. This was a messy, back-aching, nose-itching job. A ghost of a breeze that could not stir even a grass-head kept dancing round me, teasing, blowing the powder in my face whichever way I turned: I was white all over by the time I had finished, and rather cross and tired.

But that evening we went on the best trip of all. Its main purpose was to take Norman home to Canoe for the weekend. Norman had been "living in" since Monday – that is to say, he had been sleeping on a mattress on the floor of the top boathouse. The day he had brought his few possessions over he had been fetched by Buster from Canoe, and had left his own ramshackle rowboat at home.

Buster never went out in the boat without taking Jessie to act as ballast; this time he had a good load of it, for Frances and I went too. At sundown we filed down the front path in holiday mood. Even after such a gay week, I found the arrival at the water's edge as exciting as an arrival at the theatre. Life at the Harolds' was so simple that its major thrills came from events which a city- dweller might consider small and dull. Back in England I had been thrilled by hunts, dances, and visits to the theatre; but none of these had given me the very special joy that I found here in the rare days in town, the Sunday trips up the lake, the arrival of the weekly mail, or even the sight of the cougar's footprint. Now, instead of the endless after-supper routine of dishpans and kettles, we had before us a prospect of sunset and starlight, speed and silence, freedom and peace. What more could one desire?

We all helped to push the long, slender boat down its rollers into the water, where it arrived with a whisper of pleasure. Buster brought it round to the wharf, that wobbly plank of an exciting wharf, the threshold of every important event, whether tragic or happy. One by one we stepped down into the boat and settled ourselves. Of course,

Norman had to sit at Buster's end, and we women-folk together in the bows to chat of feminine things. So maddeningly conventional and old-fashioned. Yesterday at the Lesters' it had been just the same: all the men standing in the back kitchen to talk farming, and the women sitting politely in the living-room talking clothes and illnesses and babies. Today, as usual, we did chat of feminine things – at least, Jessie did.

Buster started the motor, and we rushed instantly into the glorious swooshing curve which I loved so much. The boathouse became part of the view, nestling under the row of trees which fringed the shore and hid the farm; then in a moment the whole scene vanished as we rounded the point and passed the creek mouth where the little Jerseys so valiantly did their swimming.

As we left the bay Spruce Hills came gradually into view, gliding out from behind the point in solemn procession. Deepest blue they were, duskily mysterious, and superb in their unconcerned pride. Behind them, the evening brightness was already fading in the sky.

The boat was paying out a fine white rope of wake, which lay at first in a smooth arc on the water, but was pulled taut as we swung clear of the point and headed out towards the far shore. Except for this straight and gleaming trail, the water was unbroken: under the western sky, between pine-clad headlands, and far off into the darkening east it lay, satin-smooth, full of soft gleams and velvet shadows. It caressed the boat below my hand, and stretched away and away to the great mountains on every side: it was at once intimate and infinite. Like God, I thought.... I could think that night, too, for Jessie and Frances were talking happily together. Usually, Jessie would keep up an unnecessary running commentary on the beauties which surrounded us;

she would keep asking questions which required answers, and I would try to reply brightly without losing hold of one of those precious moments. But now I sat quietly, just looking and looking, letting the great stillness soak into me.

It was dark when we got back, and Dr. and Mrs. Harold had gone to bed. We sat up late: Buster and Jessie and Frances drank glasses of milk, and we all munched on buns. The oil-lamp cast a circle of warm, yellow light on and around the table. I lay back in an easy chair with the sentimental Tess lying more or less all over me, a heap of fur and friendliness. Everyone was tired but comfortable, hungry but within easy reach of the home made, sticky buns. "Lucky us," said Jessie.

At midnight we went to bed. Frances and I "went along" together, going one behind the other on the narrow path to avoid the dew-laden grass. We had a companionable little chat through the partition.

In my hut I had a special surprise all to myself. As I hung my jeans over a dress on the back of the chair, boom, something flew out of the dress, circled my head twice, and shot up onto a beam. An enormous and hideously noisy insect, ugh! I wasn't going to sleep with that for company. Very cautiously I went to investigate. The thing boomed off to another beam and this time I saw it properly: it was my little humming-bird, the one who used to come to the delphiniums and stare at me through the screen! How rude of me to have felt so horrified. He was very frightened, but sleepiness made him slow and stupid, and he was not hard to catch.

I took him in my hands, warm, throbbing and incredibly small: I swear he weighed no more than a head of thistledown. He shone with iridescent greens in the lamplight. I put him on a fence-post outside, and he clung tightly to the rough wood. I felt it an honour that he had chosen to sleep in my dress, and was sorry I had disturbed him.

Nobody disturbed me: I drifted off to sleep with my head full of fresh memories. The swift movement of the boat still seemed to swing me along through the night; and in my mind I could still see the ferocious, over-hanging bulk of Bastion Mountain, outlined sharply against a glowing yellow sky, brooding blackly over a lake of liquid silver.

David , Frances, Jessie , Buster   "Gopher Point"

"Sunday," I wrote in my diary, "was a wonderful last day for Frances and me." The diary records the bare facts: that we went on a boat trip as far as Deep Gorge (but still not to Mosquito Creek); that David turned up and was persuaded at the last minute to accompany us; and that Dr. and Mrs.

Harold were obliged to stay at home and look after each other, for they had given up these all-day trips long since. It goes on to state that we had a picnic in the rain, fished without success till four o'clock, and paid several visits on the way home; and that we arrived back after dark having dropped David a mile east of the farm, to bring the cows home by flashlight.

But most of that "wonderful day" has dissolved in the mists of memory: only a few scenes stand out clearly. I recall how after the picnic Buster took photographs of us all. We arranged ourselves in attitudes of mild photographic affection, and David put his arm around my shoulders. When Frances got out her own camera Buster joined the group. "If Dave can have her shoulders, I'll have her ankles," he said, and acted accordingly. Cameras have strange effects on strict, old-fashioned codes of behaviour.

The next thing I remember clearly is helping David with the cows. He had brought them successfully home but could not induce them to enter the cow-barn. I went out in the dark to hear hooves pattering and skidding in and out of the alley way, long terrified blowings, and a desperate, pleading voice of David: "Come on, bossies, come on!" He was tearing back and forth waving the flashlight; black shadows leaped here and there, and the brilliant beam lit up now a pair of horns, now a heaving flank, now a big, frightened Jersey eye. It never by any chance shone in through the cow-barn door: there seemed to be a wall of solid darkness in there. David was the only one who could see where he was going. He did not realize that the cows were dazzled by the light and afraid of the fluttering dark. I asked for the torch and laid it on the floor behind one of the horse stalls, with the beam pointing up the gangway towards the far end of the barn; and we drove the cows in in a matter of a few minutes. David thought I had worked some kind of miracle.

The first of the farewells took place that night. David came out to watch me milking Jenny, and his eyes were sad.

"May I write to you sometimes, Lavender?"

"Of course, David; I hope you will. And I'll write to you."

"That sure would be nice."

"But I'll be seeing you again," I assured him, "when I come back to Salmon Arm.

This isn't goodbye."

"I guess not," said David, brightening a little.

We were alone in the cow-barn. The lamp hung high and crooked on a harness peg; two moths whirred around it and bumped heavily against its glass panes. The cows breathed in their shadowy stalls and the soft night whispered outside. Buster, tactful soul, was late in coming. David waited until I had finished milking Jenny and weighing her milk; then he held both my hands and wished me luck on my travels, and made me promise to send him my address.

As I watched him walk out into the night I was sad for myself and sorry for him; yet I was glad he had not kissed me, and my own coldness astonished me.

Early on Monday morning there was a nip in the air which presaged September, and the sun shone on puffy white clouds which lay low on the mountainsides. The lake steamed with golden mist, sharp trees speared out of the whiteness at unearthly heights, and the skirted mountains lifted their proud, dark heads into a filmy sky. The beauty of it all caught at the heart and destroyed the power of words. As I drove the cows out into the brilliant haze I turned to Buster, and realized that this was my first and last opportunity of showing him my heart. All I could do was bury my face against his shoulder and say: "This is the last time I shall milk for you." but he was kind. He put his arms round me and spoke to me as to a child: "You mustn't cry." I had no tears. Perhaps he did not understand, but he comforted nevertheless.

Later, when the morning sun blazed down out of a blue sky and chased the last wraiths of mist between the highest trees, everybody assembled by the wharf for some final photographs. Frances took hers first. Jessie, Buster and I stood on the plank, and the two old people sat on a log at our feet. Buster put his arm about my waist and there was kindness is his touch but no trace of desire.

When he took the camera himself, Jessie put on arm round Frances and the other round me. After that it was time to go. The Doctor shook my hand and said I'd be mad if I stayed in the city long. Mrs. Harold kissed me and said, "You will come back; you must come back." I promised them I'd surprise them one day: if I couldn't get a lift by boat I'd walk right round the lake by Tappen and sneak up on them from the woods. Frances said her fond farewells to them, and I was glad I had somebody else to share a poignancy that would have been too much to bear alone.

Mrs. Herald, Dr. H. , Jessie

Then came the familiar settling into the boat, the starting of the motor, the rush of speed and the white arc of foam upon the water. How quickly these two dear figures dwindled into the distance; stout Mrs. Harold with her bent old knees and her bent old back, standing as straight as she could and waving a white handkerchief; and the thin old man by her side smiling his toothless smile and waving his yellow straw hat – two people I had grown to love. I waved, Frances waved, and they waved back again and again – two small, valiant figures on their own beach in front of their own brave acres which they themselves had wrested from the relentless wilderness. We waved yet again, and two mere dots waved back – dots standing on the white shore with the forest rising up behind them to the red rocks and the blue sky. One last wave, then the point blotted them out, and there was only the lake and the woods and the hot sunshine. Buster leaned forward and tapped me on the shoulder. "Would you like to try your hand at steering?" he asked.

I changed places with him and he showed me how to steer and how to look after the motor; then he kept watch over me and encouraged me with an occasional word of praise. I looked past Frances and Jessie, fixing my eye on the distant white wharf of Canoe, and obeyed Buster's instructions. It was a relief to forget the sadness of retreating and to face forwards again: I was grateful to Buster for his gesture. I began to believe that he had after all understood my feelings in the cow-barn that morning. It was as if he were saying: "I know how you feel; I feel the same was toward you but I have no words with which to tell you."

When we arrived in Canoe, Buster and Jessie helped Frances and me up the street with our luggage, and waited to see us into the "bus"; but it was down on the wharf that we said our real goodbyes. Jessie kissed Frances and me and made us both promise to come again. She made me feel that I would be no less keenly missed than her old friend. I said what I hoped were the right words to her; but when Buster took my hand I could find none at all. "Oh, Buster, I just don't know what to say," I faltered.

He held my hand more tightly and looked straight into my eyes. "Your actions speak for themselves," he said; and I knew that he had understood.

The crowded old car that was called a bus swept me away from a lovely but completed part of my life, towards – I knew not what.

CHAPTER THIRTY-SEVEN

When I had seen Frances off on her train I went to Mrs. Meeks "Beauty Shoppe." but the door was locked. Half a dozen cars stood outside in the parking-lot, but hers was not among them. There was no reply when I telephoned her home and for a while I knew despair. No Meeks, no Harolds, no work to do! I began to wonder why I had ever left the farm, life seemed so empty and flat without it. I went to the hotel and treated myself to a civilized bath, but for once even that luxury held no delight for me.

Outside, the sun beat relentlessly down on the dull, square blocks of the houses, and glared up from the dusty white roads. The Meeks must have gone to Kelowna: if they did not return today, I decided , I would leave for Vancouver tomorrow without waiting to see them. Now I had left the farm I must at all costs go on with my journey: I could not bear this miserable, empty waiting. In front of the station the gaudy signboard seemed to mock me from a closed past: "Welcome to Salmon Arm, the Jewel of the Shuswap Valley." Today I preferred to look at the tall, many-armed signpost beside it, with the topmost board that pointed bravely westwards bearing the legend VANCOUVER 315.

After a lonely lunch in a cafe I rang the Meeks again, and, to my amazement, got an answer.

"We have been here all day," said Mrs. Meek. "We must both have been outside when you rang before. Yes, we did go to Kelowna, but we got back a day earlier than we expected, and thought we'd both have the extra day off all the same."

She insisted that I come and spend a night with them, and within half an hour had arrived in the car to fetch me. She and Mr. Meek were eager to hear all my news and tell me more about their beloved Coast, and I soon forgot to be depressed. I washed some clothes and spread them on the long grass at the edge of the lawn, where they were bone dry in less than an hour. Mrs. Meek played the piano, and made me play to her, then we all sat on the verandah drinking long glasses of delicious canned apple-juice straight from the refrigerator.

Those two were kindness itself. Mrs. Meek made up the bed in the Monkey-house for me for that night, and Mr. Meek, who knew of a reasonably cheap hostel in Vancouver, went to the telephone and fixed up a room for me for the following night. Nothing was too much trouble. They discussed my plans as excitedly as if they were coming too. "I wish we were," said Mrs. Meek.

Next morning we were all up early, and the Meeks dropped me at the station on their way to work. They both gave me messages for Den. "Here's his telephone number," said Mrs. Meek. "You will get in touch with him right away, I hope? He'd be disappointed if you didn't; and he may have found you a job, I know he's been looking pretty hard."

I was in the train all day long, and knew no more regrets, but only excitement. I was so pleased at the idea of seeing Den again that I hardly dared let myself think about it; I concentrated instead on the scenery. For an hour or two I watched lakes slipping past the window, lovely replicas of Shuswap Lake, reflecting timber-covered, red-cragged mountains similar to Mount Ida. Then the timber thinned out, and soon the train was following a river through a vast, barren country where the parched hills were sandy brown under the blue sky, and where nothing grew but the drab, grey sagebrush.

It was grand to be travelling again, and my old westward urge began to grip me as strongly as ever. "I really am going to see the Pacific," I told myself, and that became my one ambition. The entrancing thought of it echoed rhythmically in my head: "To see the Pacific, to see the Pacific, to see the Pacific Ocean."

After its long sojourn in the arid lands our river joined the Fraser, and soon we plunged into the Fraser Canyon. For hours we crept between the feet of an inexhaustible procession of grand snowy mountains, and gazed up at more and yet more terrifying cliffs. Below us, between huge tree, we could see the white water hurtling and swirling on its way to the ocean. The Canadian Pacific and Canadian National railways run near the bottom of the beetling precipices, one on either side of the river; but the road is high up on the canyon side, often nothing more than a perilous ledge. Now and again I glimpsed a microscopic bus up there, crawling insect-like round some terrible bend: and I resolved that nobody would ever persuade me to do this journey by road.

At last we came out into the broad, lower Fraser Valley, now a wide, flooding expanse of river with a back-ground of mountains and a soft smudging of trees. The water was opalescent under the fading pink sunset light; and just before the lights were switched on in the train I saw the silver gleam of a young moon.

It was after eleven when we arrived: all I saw of Vancouver that night was the station, a mass of neon lighting, the hostel reception desk and my own drab little bedroom. I fell asleep the moment my head touched the pillow.

CHAPTER THIRTY-EIGHT

Half past six the following evening found me waiting nervously in the lounge of the hostel; Den was taking me out to dinner. I had telephoned him at lunch-time and he had insisted I should come out with him that very evening. "I think I have found something for you in the way of a job," he had said. "Tell you all about it when we meet."

I was far more excited than justified by the faint possibility of a job; also, I was unreasonably worried about my clothes. A short cotton sun-dress seemed hardly appropriate for a dinner-date, but everything else I had was still crumpled from packing and I had been unable to get anyone in the hostel to lend me an iron. "Wear anything," Den had gaily told me, "only it must be okay for walking: I'm going to show you the sights." So there was no cause for worry; but I did worry, ridiculously.

It had been a strange day. I had been unable to settle to job-hunting, or even to sight-seeing, and had whiled away the hot hours with shop-gazing and exploring. I had marvelled at the the street- cars, at the city crowds, at the enormous number of cinemas, and, most of all, at the lovely, blue-green mountains that rose incongruously but comfortingly over the great, noisy canyons of the streets. But I had not given these things my full attention. All the morning I had been impatient, and all the afternoon I had been strangely elated. "There is nothing," I told myself severely, "to be elated about." but the feeling persisted, and I knew it had very little to do with the city or the job.

Suddenly the door opened and Den walked in. He was even taller than I had remembered, and very handsome in grey flannels and a navy blue blazer. The little room seemed immensely long as I walked through it to meet him. He grinned down at me as he took my hand. "My, you do look well!" he said. "Harold's farm must have suited you."

Outside, to my amazement, he had a smart little car waiting. "But I didn't think you had a - " I began.

"I haven't," he said. "It's a U-Drive."

"A U-Drive?"

"Yes, U-Drive, you drive yourself. I hired it," he explained.

Over an expensive dinner in a restaurant he told me about the job. It was outdoor work, in the experimental gardens of the Faculty of Agriculture at the University. It sounded ideal to me: nice boss, reasonable hours, and far higher pay that what I had been accustomed to.

And so near Den! I grew more and more excited.

"Buy for Heaven's sake don't bank on it," Den warned. "It's only a possibility. I think it'll come off, but I don't know. I should hear tomorrow, so hang on till then."

"Den, I don't know why you do all this for me."

"Oh, it's nothing. I like to help somebody who's got guts."

UBC Science Building. Vancouver B.C.

We drove over a long bridge, turned into the setting sun and followed the shore. For miles the road was lined with houses and gardens, and on every lawn a revolving spray sent silver curves patterning over the grass. Then the houses were gone, and the road lay under high, bushy cliffs alongside a sandy beach where the high-water mark was strewn with monster driftwood logs. Across the water dark mountains brooded, and far behind, at the head of the inlet, a proud line of skyscrapers glowed pink in front of the city haze. A steamer was coming in, white against the mountain forests, and three tugs were going out.

Now we were climbing into the sunset. Wooded cliffs dropped away below us to jade-green water; while ahead, behind a grill of bare, lofty firs, a great heaped fire of cloudlets burned suddenly from gold to red.

At the top of the hill the road curved into a canyon of trees and we had no view at all. But a moment later Den drove the car up onto a grassy patch beside the road. "Now!" he said. "You wanted to see the Pacific? Quick, before the red goes out of the sky!"

We jumped out, locked the car, and were plunging into the woods in less time than it takes to tell. Den led the way to a path which dived steeply between giant fir-tree boles, and we ran down helter-skelter, jumping tree-roots and slithering in the pine- needles. We could hardly have come down more quickly on skis. I had no idea how far we were going, I had eyes only for Den's form bounding down in front of me, and the dark ground flying up towards my feet.

All at once there were rocks instead of earth, the trees ended and the glowing sky unveiled. We

were on a lonely beach facing due west, and before us the great, wide sea was a rippling red mirror to the glory of the clouds. My Pacific Ocean! A row of dim mountain shapes showed below the sunset, but they did not spoil my tremendous sense of satisfaction. My westward urge was at last fulfilled.

I followed Den down over the rocks to the curving white fringe of the sea, and there, when I had recovered my breath, I tried to tell him how I felt. "It is amazing," I said. "I seem to have found everything I have dreamed of: my lake, my mountains, my Wild West farm with exactly the right people living on it, my sight of the Pacific. I have found everything, except -" and then I blurted out something I had never intended to say – Except – oh, everything except you, Den."

Den did not answer, but only stared at the sea, his back to me. All the joy of the evening died within me in that moment. We stood in awkward silence, and even as we stood the fires of sunset went out, leaving ashen clouds and a sudden chill in the air; the gay colours faded from the sea.

I was miserable, and bitterly disappointed, though I was not quite sure what I had been expecting. I was disgusted with myself for having spoken, yet I knew I could not have done otherwise, for I was still in the grip of that strange power which had been impelling me ever since I had begun my westward journey. That was a power altogether outside my ken; whether it had been driving me towards happiness or disaster I had neither known nor cared: I had been as helpless before it as thistledown before the wind, and, until now, strangely contented in my helplessness.

But now I was horrified, not only at myself for having spoken so impulsively, but also at the overwhelming truth of what I had said: I did indeed love Den. Until I had told him I had not known – not consciously known – that I had loved him all these weeks. While I was in Salmon Arm I had not understood that some of the extra glory of my surroundings came from within me because of this love; neither had I understood that my mountains, my lake, even my dear Harold family, were for me only the means to an end, no more than half the fulfillment of my dream.

Lacking understanding, I had often wondered at the restlessness that had shadowed my contentment and had called me away from the haven I had found. I had even imagined I had protected myself from loving: had I not been cold to David, and had I not stepped away when Den had touched me, that time among the hummingbirds in the orchard, when we had come down from his mountain?

But now I knew, and it occurred to me that some deep, inner part of me had known all along, of my love. An empty love! "Now the moment has come," I thought bitterly. "This is the final encounter towards which my trusted fates have been forcing me: and for what?" I wished vehemently that I had resisted them at every turn.

Tears stung in my eyes as I turned and walked back across the rocks and up the path towards the trees. I could hear Den following a little way behind, but dared not look back. Darkness was gathering under the great firs, and I stumbled once or twice, but I did not slacken my pace. I had just started up the first steep part of the path when Den spoke at last: "Hey, steady there!"

He sounded much closer than I had thought, and I looked round in surprise. Although he was very near me, the pale afterglow in the west threw his head into silhouette and I could not see his face; yet somehow I could feel his eyes holding mine, and I did not turn away again.

He spoke my name once, just that, but all tenderness was in his voice. Then, amazingly yet inevitably, his arms were closing around me and his head bowing down over mine; I was able to see his face again, and I remember looking up for an instant into the warmest, tenderest smile I had ever known. Then there was no more seeing, no more speaking. I felt my hands moving unbidden over the strength of his shoulders, journeying up the taut tendons of his neck and into his hair, speaking for me without fear. Misunderstanding fled with speech; and by that ancient and universal language, the delicate, untutored language of touch, a bridge was built between his loneliness and mine. We both loved, oh! We loved each other!

I opened my eyes at the other end of eternity, and saw over Den's shoulder a golden half-moon sliding from the clouds and the black branches, dropping endways on towards the mountains on Vancouver Island; and the dull sea sparkled again, from those far mountains to the rocks below us, with fragments of golden light.

"I didn't know," Den was saying. "Oh, my darling, I didn't know."

"I'm not sure whether I knew myself, till now," I whispered.

Gently he released me and led me up the steep path, going in front himself and holding my hand in both of his behind his back, because the way was too narrow for us to walk abreast. We climbed in almost reverent silence, treading gently on the worn earth, feeling instinctively for tree-root ridges, and brushing past cool ferns. All around us gigantic trees grew vertically out of the steep hillside and soared to majestic heights. They were magnificently indifferent to human life. No breath of wind stirred in their dark branches; the only sound came from far below us, from hidden waves on the hidden beach: hush, hush, hush.

At the top of the path, where the trees drew aside like curtains to reveal a great stretch of the sea, we found a level place to sit, for we needed to talk. Our kiss, and the knowledge it had brought, had raised us too suddenly to dizzy heights within ourselves: we were exultant but still puzzled, and felt the need of ordinary words. Speech came naturally now, releasing us from tension and strengthening our new understanding. We confided in each other our secret fears and bewilderment's, our hopes and special joys; and we found that the circles of our personalities and tastes overlapped again and again, like the ripples from two stones dropped into a pond.

But at last we fell silent, the moon slid slowly, slantingly across the sky, and vanished behind the Island mountains. Stars shone, like patches of daisies, in scattered groups between the clouds, and the night air was warm and quiet and tender.

I stared into the night, and it seemed that I understood. For the first time in my life I understood the trees, the night, the stars, the universe, and how they and Den and I were one. Because I saw the meaning of The Sleeping Beauty, the significance of the awakening kiss. To be awake is to be aware, and to be aware is to be wholly present, both physically and spiritually, in life; and how can this be, until one has known what all bodies and souls were surely made for, physical and spiritual love?"

From the bottom of my heart I thanked my kind Fate for having brought me so insistently to this end. And it was with the same deep sense of gratitude that I remembered how this same Fate had led me to the Harolds' farm: for there I had learnt the love of beauty and the value of silence, the true meaning of "living close to the earth," and the way to reach happiness by sheer hard work. "For the rest of my life I shall be glad I worked for the Harolds," I said aloud.

"They must be wonderful people," said Den. "I've heard so much about them but I've never seen them. What are they really like?"

I tried to describe them to him: Mrs. Harold bent double over the strawberries or over the stove; Jessie scraping the last atom of food from a saucepan into the cats' dish, or dressed for town, plastic triangle tied like a sail over her enormous straw hat. I told him of the Doctor with his gleaming turquoise eyes, his wheezy, toothless laugh and his barely audible stories at table; and of Buster, woolly-haired and gentle, being as patient with the uncouth

Norman as he was with his animals, and being repaid as well for his patience. I tried to tell him everything about them that I had been unable to convey in letters.

When at last I stopped, Den said:

"But I always gathered the old man was a bit of a devil?"

"He's getting old now, you know. But I believe he was pretty fierce when he was younger.

What have you heard about him?"

"Oh, I can't remember now. Something about beating his wife, and refusing to let his sons have a tractor for the farm, I guess. I don't know. It's all so long ago, and I've been away from home so much. Anyway, one has to take gossip like that with a big pinch of salt."

"I can't imagine Dr. Harold beating his wife, they are devoted to each other," I said. "And as for the tractor, it is the last thing Buster wants. None of his friends can persuade him to get one." "One has to be so careful not to judge people by hearsay," Den said. "One has to find out about them for oneself."

"Well, I found out plenty," I said, "and I think the Harolds are good through and through."

"I think so, too. I would like very much to meet them," said Den. "Will you introduce me one day?"

I promised I would. "I think you'll like them; and they'll like you, I know. Jessie will call you a'woodsy sort of boy.'"

"Oh?"

"Because you love trees and animals and birds, like they do," I explained. "The 'boy' part

because you are under fifty," I added; and we both laughed.

"It depressed me sometimes, when Mrs. Harold lumped Jessie and me together as 'you young people,'" I said. "I believe that was one of the reasons I didn't stay, I was terrified of getting like Jessie, angular and wispy and always talking about neighbours' illnesses!"

"What rubbish!" scolded Den. "And how unfair to Jessie."

I felt small, and rightly so; and we were silent awhile.

Then Den asked: "Do you think Buster will get married?"

"No, I'm quite sure he won't. He is such a confirmed bachelor now, I don't think he would want to change. In any case Jessie is his partner: he is always calling her his 'better half.' I believe he would consider marriage a disloyalty to her, and I have an idea she feels the same about him.

Though I wish they'd both married years ago. It seems sheer crime for there to be such nice, special people with no possibility of descendants. People like the Harolds, just becoming extinct.... I think it's a shame.

Den said nothing for a few minutes, then he said slowly: "The important thing is happiness. Are they happy?"

I thought of the Doctor watching the boats on his beloved lake; of Mrs. Harold, pride twinkling in her eyes, urging Buster on to more and better stories; I thought of Jessie with her sketching, and her inability to understand how people could want to go 'to the movies, when there are so many wonderful things to do and see in the country.' I thought of Buster, slow and wise and thorough, cultivating his land in his own old-fashioned way and reaping his own fine, satisfying crops.

"Yes, they are happy," I replied. "I am quite, quite sure they are happy." "Well, that's okay, then," said Den, and I knew he was right.

After that we talked no more, but sat hand in hand there at the cliff-top, peacefully silent together.

My thoughts trailed back to an afternoon in early May, when I had found British Columbia in my atlas and had studied the strange, printed names – Golden, Revelstoke, Kamloops, Vancouver. "Soon," I had said then, in a flash of prophetic excitement, "soon, one or two little patches on this map are going to mean a whole chunk of life for me. Familiar scenes, they will call up: beloved mountain shapes, place-names with the poetry of association in them, and friends so close that I won't be able to imagine a time when I had not known them." How true that had been: a prophecy fulfilled indeed!

Sitting there with Den, I became more and more conscious of this sense of fulfillment. All the summer I had been living, half-puzzled, according to an unknown plan; now the plan was lived out, its structure revealed. I remembered how once I had felt as though I were compelled to live through a previously written book: well, I had done so. Here I was, at the last page, with every sentence behind me, faithfully copied into my own living memory.

But now I must plot my life myself. Suddenly I felt very small and weak. How could I do it? Spoilt by weeks of pleasant towing by the invisible tug of Fate, how could I navigate my own small boat again? I had forgotten how to sail alone.

At that moment, as if he had heard my thoughts, dear Den kissed both my eyes.

"Come, we must go now," he said. "How about you come sailing with me tomorrow?" I would indeed!

We got up and walked to the edge of the cliff. The waves of the Pacific rolled in below us, waves from Hawaii, China and Japan, rolling from the Far East across the back of the world to break gently, paradoxically, under the tall firs of the far West Coast.

"The end of my journey," I said.

But Den's arm tightened around me. "The beginning of ours."

THE END

Photo Gallery:

Buster, Norman Lundy, Den. Mrs. H., Dr. H. Jessie, self. (Pat), (Nancy).

Self ,Winter 1957 Canoe B.C

David with our son (Timothy) 1957

Tim, Self, Peter, Jennie.
(Lavender and David's three Children and her self 1966 @ Athabasca Glacier)

Thank you for reading my mother's story,
Timothy H. Birmingham
March, 2016

www.ingramcontent.com/pod-product-compliance
Lightning Source LLC
Chambersburg PA
CBHW031615160426
43196CB00006B/139